The SAGE Guide to Writing in Corrections

Sara Miller McCune founded SAGE Publishing in 1965 to support the dissemination of usable knowledge and educate a global community. SAGE publishes more than 1000 journals and over 800 new books each year, spanning a wide range of subject areas. Our growing selection of library products includes archives, data, case studies and video. SAGE remains majority owned by our founder and after her lifetime will become owned by a charitable trust that secures the company's continued independence.

Los Angeles | London | New Delhi | Singapore | Washington DC | Melbourne

The SAGE Guide to Writing in Corrections

Steven Hougland

Florida Sheriffs Association

Jennifer M. Allen

Nova Southeastern University

SAGE

Los Angeles | London | New Delhi
Singapore | Washington DC | Melbourne

SAGE

FOR INFORMATION:

SAGE Publications, Inc.
2455 Teller Road
Thousand Oaks, California 91320
E-mail: order@sagepub.com

SAGE Publications Ltd.
1 Oliver's Yard
55 City Road
London EC1Y 1SP
United Kingdom

SAGE Publications India Pvt. Ltd.
B 1/I 1 Mohan Cooperative Industrial Area
Mathura Road, New Delhi 110 044
India

SAGE Publications Asia-Pacific Pte. Ltd.
18 Cross Street #10-10/11/12
China Square Central
Singapore 048423

Printed in the United States of America

ISBN: 978-1-5443-6455-1

This book is printed on acid-free paper.

Acquisitions Editor: Jessica Miller
Editorial Assistant: Sarah Manheim
Production Editor: Jyothi Sriram and Gagan Mahindra
Copy Editor: Lana Todorovic-Arndt
Typesetter: Hurix Digital
Proofreader: Sarah J. Duffy
Cover Designer: Candice Harman
Marketing Manager: Jillian Ragusa

19 20 21 22 23 10 9 8 7 6 5 4 3 2 1

Brief Contents

Detailed Contents

Preface

As practitioners in probation and policing, we saw many reports that did not provide enough information to make a case for court prosecution or treatment and rehabilitation. As educators, we have seen students in criminal justice struggle with writing citations and referencing, and understanding the processes and procedures of criminal justice without seeing actual reports that mark the progression of a case through the system or the creation of an academic paper. This supplemental text focuses on teaching students how to write in the academic setting, while introducing them to a number of other writing tools, such as memos, emails, resumes, and letters. The goal is to interweave professional and applied writing, academic writing, and information literacy, with the result being a stronger, more confident report writer and student in criminal justice.

There are a couple challenges to writing in criminal justice: (1) Criminal justice practitioners fail to write for an audience and (2) the use of generic report templates. First, to write effectively, the writer must consider the audience's understanding of the topic and the audience's needs and use of the information. Most practitioners fail to consider that they have an audience beyond their immediate supervisor. As such, reports typically lack detail, are filled with slang and jargon, and are structured in a manner often confusing to those without a criminal justice background. Next, most practitioners are taught to use templates for crime types and court documents. In other words, every burglary report will follow the same format with a simple adjustment of the case facts. The same is true for other common crime types. So details may be missed or omitted because they do not "fit" the template.

Instructors also sometimes struggle with two issues that are shared by students: (1) writing for fact and (2) brevity. Students and faculty are taught throughout their academic careers to write to page-length requirements. In criminal justice reports, there is not a page-length requirement, and the writing process requires the writer to say what needs to be said factually and succinctly. Thus, students have to train themselves to identify the facts and to learn how to write only what is tangible in a report. Instructors have to find a way to teach these skills, while introducing critical thinking and information literacy. This can be a challenge for everyone involved.

Approach

Universities have historically supported intensive courses in writing and have encouraged writing in the discipline across the various academic fields. However, how this has been accomplished is not always clear and varies tremendously from school to school. Sometimes, writing is taught almost exclusively in English courses, while other times, it includes the efforts of individual criminal justice departments. Regardless of the approach, we believe that criminal justice departments have a responsibility to focus on teaching applied writing to their students because writing is an essential skill in this field. In the process of teaching applied writing, instructors can also prepare students to write well academically by introducing information literacy, critical thinking in writing, and the American Psychological Association (APA) style.

The first chapter of this text focuses on the basics of writing by introducing common grammar errors and the types of writing projects commonly seen in academia and the field of criminal justice. The second chapter introduces information literacy and digital literacy to students. Chapter 3 provides information on pretrial reports, presentence investigation reports, contact sheets, and revocation reports, all written by pretrial officers, and probation and parole officers. Chapter 4 continues to focus on report writing in corrections by discussing correctional incident reports. Memos, letters, emails, resumes, and cover letters are described in Chapter 5, along with examples of each. Chapter 6 focuses on plagiarism and APA formatting along with other types of writing styles that students may use in the college setting. The final chapter, Chapter 7, concentrates on the academic research paper by providing students a format to use and information on how to read a scholarly article.

The chapters are enhanced with other features such as:

- Chapter summaries
- Narrative and descriptive examples
- Questions for consideration and critical thinking
- In the News reports supporting the material discussed
- Applied exercises
- Examples from common documents used in pretrial reporting, probation, and parole.

Acknowledgments

Even though this is the first edition of the text, we have several individuals to thank for their contributions. We thank the following reviewers of the manuscript for their many helpful suggestions:

Anita Lavorgna, University of Southampton

Bobbie Ticknor, Valdosta State University

Brittany Rodriguez, Tarleton State University

Bryn Herrschaft-Eckman, PhD, Temple University

Carrie Maloney, East Stroudsburg University

Charles Bell, Illinois State University

Christina Mancini, PhD, Virginia Commonwealth University, Wilder School of Government and Public Affairs

Claudia Cox, Institute of Criminal Justice Studies, University of Portsmouth

Elizabeth B. Perkins, PhD, Morehead State University

Iryna Malendevych, University of Central Florida

Dr. Jean Dawson, Franklin Pierce University

Jeanne Subjack, Southern Utah University

Jeffery Dennis, Minnesota State University

Joel. M. Cox, Liberty University

Julie Brancale, Western Carolina University

Karen Clark, PhD, University of Arizona

Kenneth Whitman, Alabama A&M University

Dr. Mercedes Valadez, Division of Criminal Justice, California State University, Sacramento

Milton C. Hill, PhD, Stephen F. Austin State University

R. Neal McIntyre, Valdosta State University

Nick Zingo, California State University, Northridge

Ray Nickson, Fresno Pacific University

Renee D. Lamphere, UNC Pembroke

Selena M. Respass, Miami Dade College

Shana L. Maier, Widener University

Stephen J. Koonz, MA, LMSW, Department of Sociology, SUNY Oneonta

Tara Lulla, University of North Dakota

Tiffany J. Samsel, Rowan University

About the Authors

Steven Hougland is a Research Coordinator with the Florida Sheriffs Association. He is formerly an associate professor of criminal justice and a retired law enforcement officer with 30 years of policing experience at the state and local level. Dr. Hougland has published in the areas of police use of force and law enforcement accreditation.

Jennifer M. Allen is a full professor at Nova Southeastern University in the School of Criminal Justice. She has worked with juveniles in detention, on probation, and with those victimized by abuse and neglect. Dr. Allen has served on advisory boards for Big Brother/Big Sister mentoring programs, Rainbow Children's Home, domestic violence/sexual assault programs, and teen courts. Dr. Allen has published in the areas of restorative justice, juvenile delinquency and justice, youth programming, police crime, and police administration and ethics. She is also the co-author of *Criminal Justice Administration: A Service Quality Approach, Juvenile Justice: A Guide to Theory, Policy, and Practice, The Sage Guide to Writing in Criminal Justice, The Sage Guide to Writing in Law Enforcement (forthcoming), and The Sage Guide to Writing in Research Methods (forthcoming)*.

CHAPTER 1

The Basics of Writing

There is an adage in criminal justice that "if it's not in writing, it didn't happen." This means that criminal justice documents must provide enough details to explain what actually happened at a scene or during an incident or court hearing. Missing details or information that is written vaguely may result in a case being dismissed. Further, a poorly written report could open the door for a mistrial, a not guilty verdict, or the criminal justice worker may appear to have made up the details or to be unsure of the reported details when testifying on the stand. Therefore, it is important that those working in criminal justice understand the complexities of writing quality reports.

Corrections officers are required to write many different types of narrative and descriptive documents. In corrections, the basic incident report documents the officer's or inmate's activity; records the actions and testimony of victims, suspects, and witnesses; serves as a legal account of an event; and is used for court testimony or in parole hearings. Being the best writer possible is a necessity for professionals in the criminal justice field.

The need to write well has never been more important. Relating facts about an incident and investigation goes far beyond the eyes of the supervisor and agency. A report will convict criminals, encourage the support of the community, and become a guide by which the public and the courts will measure their respect for the criminal justice system and its workers.

Additionally, corrections reports are public record in many states. As such, they are available for all to review. Attorneys, paralegals, and staff personnel on both sides of a case, as well as judges and journalists, may read criminal justice reports. Imagine writing a report that is read by a Justice of the Supreme Court!

Similarly, criminal justice professors often require students to complete writing assignments such as essays, case analyses, and legal briefs. These assignments help develop thinking skills as well as research and writing skills required in criminal justice careers.

This chapter introduces students to common writing assignments in the criminal justice and criminology classroom as well as those required in corrections.

Basic Grammar Rules

Studies suggest successful writing skills take a long time to develop. Learning to write an effective, extended text is a vastly complex process that often requires more than two decades of training. A skilled, professional writer progresses beyond writing to tell a story to crafting the narrative with the audience's interpretation of the text in mind (Kellogg, 2008). Paragraphs and sentences form the basis of the text. Writing clear, short sentences is an important element of technical writing.

Any discussion on writing begins with the sentence.

The Sentence

The sentence is comprised of a subject and a predicate, and the unit must make complete sense. In other words, a sentence must be able to stand alone as a complete thought. Sentences can be one word or a complex combination of words. Criminal justice professionals write all documents using complete sentences, usually in the first person with no slang or jargon. On occasion, corrections documents may be written in the third person, although still with complete sentences that include a subject and a predicate. Sentences should be brief with no structural, grammatical, or spelling errors. The writer must write clear, complete sentences so that the audience can easily understand the writing.

The Subject

The subject is the word that states who or what does the action or is acted upon by the verb. The subject can be expressed or implied. Rephrase the following sentences as questions to identify the subject. So, for number 1, for example, one could ask, "Who reported the crime?" The answer, of course, is the victim, and in this sentence, "victim" functions as the subject.

Examples:

1. The *victim* reported the crime.

   Who reported the crime? The victim.
2. *I* responded to the scene.
3. *I* arrested the defendant.
4. The *Corrections Officer* read the inmate his Miranda rights.
5. The *inmate* entered the cell.

If a sentence requires a subject and a predicate, can one word function as a complete sentence? Yes, if that word is a command. In a command, the subject is the implied or understood "you."

Examples:

1. "Stop!"

   The subject is not clearly stated, but it is implied or understood to be "you."

2. "Sit down!"
3. "Halt!"

The Verb

The verb is the word or group of words that describe what action is taking place.

Examples:

1. The Corrections Officer *drove*.
   Drove tells what action the subject (Corrections Officer) did.
2. The Corrections Officer *was dispatched* to Pod C.
   Was dispatched tells what action is taking place.
3. I *restrained* the inmate.
4. *Stop*!
   Remember the subject in a command is the implied "you."
5. I *did not respond* to the call.

Standing Alone and Making Complete Sense

A complete sentence must have a subject and a verb, and it must make complete sense. The sentence must be a complete idea; it must be able to stand alone as a complete thought.

Examples:

Incorrect 1. The officer.

The subject (officer) lacks a verb and does not make complete sense.

Incorrect 2. The officer obtained.

The subject (officer) and verb (obtained) lacks complete sense.

Correct 3. The officer obtained a witness statement. (complete sentence)

Incorrect 4. The officer moved.

The subject (officer) and verb (moved) lacks complete sense.

Correct 5. The officer moved the inmate. (complete sentence)

Incorrect 6. The Corrections Officer who responded to the pod. (incomplete sentence)

Correct 7. The Corrections Officer who responded to the pod restrained the defendant. (complete sentence)

Correct 8. The officer was working. (complete sentence)

Correct 9.	The officer worked in the control room. (complete sentence)
Correct 10.	The officer worked in the recreation yard. (complete sentence)

Exercise 1.1

Identify the subject and verb in each of the following examples:

I arrested the defendant.
I (subject) + arrested (verb).

1. The inmate entered the victim's cell.
2. The inmate smashed the victim's radio.
3. He removed a canteen card from the cell.
4. The stereo is valued at $300.00.
5. I processed the scene for evidence.
6. The inmate punched the victim in the face.
7. The inmate removed the victim's property from the cell.
8. I responded to the scene.
9. I moved the inmate.
10. I transported the defendant to Central Booking for processing.

See answers on p. 20.

Structural Errors

Some of the most common structural errors in criminal justice and academic writing are fragments, run-on sentences, and comma splices. But once identified, they are easily corrected.

Fragments

A fragment is an incomplete sentence. All of the following are fragments:

1. Entered the cell. (no subject)
2. Processed the scene. (no subject)
3. I the scene. (no verb)
4. At the scene. (no subject or verb)
5. I processed. (lacks completeness)

Fragments can be corrected in one of several ways. After identifying the missing element (subject, verb, or completeness), simply insert the missing element to complete the sentence.

Revised 1.	The defendant entered the cell.
Revised 2.	A crime scene technician processed the scene.
Revised 3.	I responded to the scene.
Revised 4.	The defendant was found at the scene.
Revised 5.	I processed the scene.

Run-On Sentences

A run-on sentence is two or more complete sentences improperly joined without punctuation.

Example 1: We arrived at the scene Corrections Officer Smith interviewed the victim.

Sentence 1: We arrived at the scene.

Sentence 2: Corrections Officer Smith interviewed the victim.

Revision Strategy 1. Create two independent sentences.

Revision 1. We arrived at the scene. Corrections Officer Smith interviewed the victim.

Revision Strategy 2. Join the independent clauses with a comma and a coordinating conjunction such as *and, but, for, nor, or, so,* or *yet*.

Revision 2. We arrived at the scene, and Corrections Officer Smith interviewed the victim.

Punctuation Alert! Always place the comma *before* the coordinating conjunction.

Revision Strategy 3. Join the independent clauses with a semicolon if they are closely related ideas.

Revision 3. We arrived at the scene; Corrections Officer Smith interviewed the victim.

Comma Splices

A comma splice is two independent clauses joined improperly with a comma.

Example 1. We arrived at the scene, Corrections Officer Smith interviewed the victim.

Revision Strategy 1. Separate the two sentences by adding a comma followed by a coordinating conjunction Corrections Officer.

Revision 1. We arrived at the scene, and Corrections Officer Smith interviewed the victim.

Punctuation

All sentences contain punctuation. Punctuation helps the audience understand the writer's meaning.

> Let's eat Grandma.
> Let's eat, Grandma.
>
> Save a life—use correct punctuation.

Commas

The most frequently and misused punctuation mark is the comma. Use a comma to join two independent clauses with a coordinating conjunction (*and, but, for, or, nor, yet, so*). The comma is always placed *before* the conjunction.

A comma is used to separate a dependent clause from an independent clause.

Examples:

1. I arrested the defendant, and I booked him into the jail.

   Two independent clauses:

   1. I arrested the defendant.
   2. I booked him into the jail.

   A comma is required before the coordinating conjunction.

2. I arrested the defendant and booked him into the jail.

   One independent clause: I arrested the defendant.

   One dependent clause: booked him into the jail. (no subject)

   A comma is not used.

More examples:

1. I interviewed the victim, and she gave a sworn statement.
2. I interviewed the victim, but she refused to give a sworn statement.

A comma is used to separate items in a list. Place a comma before the *and* at the end of the series.

Examples:

1. Deputies Smith, Jones, and White responded to the call. (correct)
2. Deputies Smith, Jones and White responded to the call. (incorrect)

Commas are also used after conjunctive adverbs (however, therefore, etc.). However, if the phrase is very short—fewer than three words—the comma may be omitted.

Examples:

1. When I responded to the call, I activated my emergency lights and siren.
2. Responding to the call, I activated my emergency lights and siren.
3. Therefore, the findings of my investigation are that no crime took place.

Commas are used to isolate an appositive (a phrase that renames the noun).

Examples:

1. The man, a white male, was arrested for theft.
2. Corrections Officer Smith, a rookie, was assigned to the midnight shift.
3. My assigned vehicle, car 1042, is a 1991 Ford LTD.

Check to see whether the commas have been placed properly by simply removing the words between the commas. If what remains is a complete sentence, the commas are correctly placed.

Example:

The man, a white male, was arrested for theft.

Remove the words between the commas: a white male.

What remains, "The man was arrested for theft" is a complete sentence.

The placement of the commas is correct.

Exercise 1.2

Place or remove commas for correct punctuation.

1. We approached the defendant and Corrections Officer Smith asked to buy a "dime."
2. We approached the defendant, and asked to buy a "dime."
3. At today's Day-Shift briefing Sergeant Jones asked for volunteers.
4. I charged the defendant with sale and delivery of cocaine, possession of cocaine and possession of drug paraphernalia.
5. Sergeant Jones the Day-Shift supervisor, asked for volunteers.
6. I arrested the defendant for shoplifting yet he denied the charge.
7. I am usually assigned to Pod D but today I am working in Pod A.
8. Today I wrote reports for burglary, theft and battery.
9. Corrections Officer Smith, an experienced drug agent made a cocaine seizure today.

See answers on p. 20.

The Semicolon

The semicolon indicates a strong relationship between two sentences.

Examples:

1. I interviewed the victim; however, she failed to provide a statement.
2. I arrested the defendant; later, I transported and booked him into the jail.

Exercise 1.3

Insert or remove semicolons for correct punctuation.

1. We responded to the call, Corrections Officer Smith wrote the report.
2. At briefing the sergeant asked for; volunteers and reports.
3. I saw the nurse treating the victim. She had a stomach wound.
4. The defendant removed the item from the shelf, she then left the store after failing to pay.
5. I am assigned to Pod C, but I primarily work the recreation yard.

See answers on p. 20.

The Colon

The colon is used to introduce a list.

Examples:

1. The defendant was charged with the following: burglary, grand theft, and criminal mischief.
   (Notice the placement of the commas in the series.)
2. Three officers responded to the call: Smith, Jones, and Harris.

Exercise 1.4

Insert colons appropriately.

1. I charged the inmate with the following, assault, battery, and theft.
2. The following attachments are provided with this report, sworn statements, and evidence form.
3. I testified on several cases today while in court 92-123456, 90-123456, and 89-123456.

See answers on p. 21.

Quotation Marks

Quotation marks are used to indicate another person's spoken or written words. They are useful in criminal justice documents to indicate statements made by suspects or defendants, responses or comments by victims or witnesses that are particularly relevant to an investigation, or anytime an important statement is made. Students also regularly use quotation marks in their academic papers. Although, it is important to remember to only quote from a source when the information cannot be paraphrased in another way, it involves statistics that must be stated exactly, or the point is so important that a student believes it must be stated exactly as the original author wrote. Students should always use quoted material sparingly and attempt to paraphrase or summarize the work as much as possible.

If the quotation is placed at the end of the sentence, a comma is placed before the opening quotation mark. A period is placed within the end quotation mark at the end of the sentence:

Examples:

1. The inmate stated, "I didn't mean to kill her."
2. I told the defendant, "You're under arrest."

If a sentence begins with a quotation, a comma is placed within the end quotation mark.

Example:

1. "I didn't mean to kill her," he said.

If a quotation mark is around a single word or group of words, the punctuation *always* goes inside the quotation mark:

Examples:

1. I asked the suspect if he knew where I could purchase a "dime," the common street reference for $10 of cocaine.
2. The victim told me he had taken LSD and was "high," so I called Medical for medical treatment.

Exercise 1.5

Punctuate the following sentences properly using quotation marks and commas as needed.

1. The victim said He stabbed me in the stomach.
2. He stabbed me in the stomach she said.
3. She said He stabbed me in the stomach, but I saw no wound.
4. The officer asked, Who attacked you?
5. Who was it who said Live and let live?

See answers on p. 21.

Plurals

Many nouns are changed to the plural form simply by adding -s or -es to the end of the noun: *Officer* becomes *officers*; *bus* becomes *buses*. Some nouns, however, form plurals irregularly by changing the spelling of the word. Some of the most common include:

man men   woman women   me us   I we

Some nouns do not change their spelling at all to form plurals: *deer*, *sheep*, *fish*, *police*.

Some nouns that have a Latin root still use the Latin form of the plural rather than the English -s. Some examples include *datum/data*, *crisis/crises*, and *memorandum/memoranda*.

Possessives

The possessive form demonstrates a relationship between two nouns.

Examples:

1. The victim's car was burglarized.
2. The defendant's rights were revoked.
3. The vehicle's tires were slashed.

If the noun is plural and ends with an s, add only an apostrophe.

Examples:

1. The victims' cars were burglarized.
2. The defendants' rights were revoked.
3. These are the victims' radios.
4. Here are the officers' guns.
5. The vehicles' tires were slashed.

Capitalization

Capitalize the names of directions when they indicate a specific location, but not when they indicate a general direction.

Examples:

1. South Carolina
2. The defendant fled south on foot.

Capitalize titles only when they precede the person's name.

Examples:

1. Colonel Smith
2. I met with the colonel.

Commonly Misused Words

Homophones are words that look and sound alike but have different meanings. The following are examples of homophones:

Its and *it's*

1. *Its* shows possession. "You can't judge a book by its cover."
2. *It's* is the contraction of *it is*.

There, *their*, and *they're*

1. *There* indicates a location. An easy way to remember this is to look for the word "here" within "there." *There* also functions as an adverb, as in "There are no more calls holding."
2. *Their* is an adjective. It describes a noun by showing that an object belongs to more than one person or thing: "Their car was burglarized," or "Here is their stolen property," or "The dogs were in their pen."
3. *They're* is the contraction of *they are*.

Lie, *lay*, *lain*: to recline

1. I will now lie down.
2. Yesterday I lay down.
3. Last week, I had also lain down.

Lay, *laid*, *laid*: to place or set down

1. I will now lay my book down.
2. He laid the gun on the ground.
3. He had already laid his gun down.

Who and *whom*

Who is used as a subject; *whom* is used as an object.

1. Who wrote the report?
2. The lieutenant asked the sergeant, "Whom did you have write this report?"

In modern, spoken English, *whom* is rarely used.

Which, *who*, and *that*

Use *which* and *that* to refer to animals and things. Always use *who* to refer to people.

1. The horses, which were kept at the stable, jumped the fence to get loose.
2. The deputies who responded to the call took 2 minutes to arrive.

Exercise 1.6

Insert the correct word.

1. A police patrol car is easily identified by (it's/its) ________ distinctive color scheme.
2. When is shift change? (It's/Its) ________ this weekend.
3. Yes, (there/their/they're) ________ are no bananas.
4. We are going over (there/their/they're) ________.
5. We found (there/their/they're) ________ stolen property.
6. (There/Their/They're) ________ going over (there/their/they're) ________.
7. I will (lie/lay/lain) ________ down now.
8. The suspect (lay/laid) ________ the gun on the ground, and the officer ordered him to (lie, lay, lain) ________ face down.
9. (Who/Whom) ________ responded to the call?
10. Corrections Officer Smith, (who/whom) ________ did you interview at the scene?
11. The people (which/who/that) ________ were arrested during the reverse sting operation were all adults.

See answers on p. 21.

The Modifier

A modifier is a word or group of words that describe a noun or a verb. Modifiers may appear before or after the word they describe, but the modifier must be logically placed to prevent confusion.

Examples:

1. Correctional Officer Smith's decision to transfer was an *important* career move.
2. The crime scene perimeter was planned *carefully* by the sergeant.

Notice that the modifiers in both sentences can be dropped without changing the meaning of the sentence.

1. Correctional Officer Smith's decision to transfer was a career move.
2. The crime scene perimeter was planned by the sergeant.

Modifiers can easily confuse readers when they are misplaced within a sentence.

Examples:

1. Suffering from a heart attack, Corrections Officer Smith found the victim at her door. (Who had the heart attack?)

Revised

1. Corrections Officer Smith found the victim at her door suffering from a heart attack.

Examples:

Misplaced 1: The female Corrections Officer, while searching the female informant, found the drugs that were sold by Deputy Smith in the woman's pants.

Revised 1: The female Corrections Officer, while searching the female informant, found the drugs in the woman's pants. The drugs were sold by Deputy Smith in the reverse sting operation.

Misplaced 2: Deputy Jones, while on routine patrol, saw the drunk driver who was arrested by Deputy Harris driving south on Kirkman Road.

Revised 2: Deputy Jones, while on routine patrol, saw the drunk driver driving south on Kirkman Road. Deputy Harris arrested the drunk driver.

Spelling

Proper spelling is a vital part of every written document. Just as improper grammar and punctuation are signs of semi-literacy, so too is improper spelling. A misspelled word screams for the reader's attention and shapes a negative image of the writer. Several misspelled words can have such a negative effect upon the reader that many will simply refuse to continue reading, finding it too difficult to understand the narrative.

Those who write by hand should keep a good dictionary nearby. When writing on a computer, do not overly rely on the spell check. While a spell

accept	attack	disturbance	misdemeanor
accurate	attorney	efficient	paraphernalia
accuse	battery	examination	receive
acquaintance	bruise	fellatio	sergeant
advisable	bureau	felony	sheriff
aggravated	burglary	foreign	subpoena
apparent	canvassed	harass	tattoo
appeal	cemetery	height	trafficking
apprehend	commit	homicide	trespass
apprehension	conceal	interrogate	trying
approximate	confidential	intoxication	unnecessary
argument	conveyance	jewelry	vicinity
armed robbery	counsel	judge	victim
arraignment	criminal	juvenile	warrant
assault	cunnilingus	lieutenant	weight
associate	discipline	marijuana	wounded

check will identify and correct misspelled words, it will fail to correct homophones. In this sentence, *four* example, the word "for" is misspelled as "four," yet a spell check program would fail to identify the error.

The box on the facing page contains is a list of some of most frequently misspelled words used in criminal justice writing.

Critical Thinking Skills, Academic Writing, and Professional Writing

Being able to identify errors in writing and to write thorough reports and interesting academic papers requires the ability to think critically. A critical thinker will write better because he or she will weed out nonessential information from written documents. Rugerrio (2008) defines critical thinking as "the process by which we test claims and arguments and determine which have merit and which do not" (p. 18). Ennis (2011) adds, "Critical thinking is reasonable, reflective thinking that is focused on deciding what to believe or do" (p. 1). Critical thinking is a foundational goal of the college experience because it is at the core of modern personal, social, and professional life (Paul, 1995). Phillips and Burrell (2009) note critical thinkers overcome biases and false assumptions that impede decision-making. As such, critical thinking prepares students for all aspects of life.

Academic writing enhances critical thinking in several key ways. It is a process that requires students to verify the credibility and biases of source material and objectively examine not just their thoughts and beliefs but also the ideas of those diametrically opposed to their own (Paul, 1995).

Critical thinking is also an essential skill in the criminal justice professions since it is a key piece of problem solving. Common writing assignments in criminal justice classes include a reflective journal, essay paper, research paper, monograph, annotated bibliography, case study, and legal analysis.

Reflective Journal

The reflective journal assignment is designed to capture a student's feelings and responses to an issue. Journals are more than a synopsis or a simple "I think" response to a question. This assignment requires students to thoroughly and critically evaluate a reading assignment by applying current theory, practice, and course materials to assess a problem, issue, or policy.

Essay Paper

A common assignment for students is the essay paper. The narrative and descriptive essay are examples that require no outside research. For these essays, students are asked to tell a story, explain a process, or describe a place or thing. The length of this essay is typically five pages or less, but length can vary according to the course and instructor.

Research Paper

Like the essay paper, the research paper is a commonly assigned project, especially in upper level courses. Here, students must conduct outside research to identify source materials that either support or refute a thesis. Students must critically analyze sources to ensure the information is from a respected and reliable source and is both current and credible. Although many students feel anxious about writing a research paper, it can be a valuable experience since "many students will continue to do research throughout their career" (Purdue Owl, 2018a).

Monograph

A monograph is an in-depth study of a single subject written by faculty or scholars for an academic audience (Eastern Illinois University, 2016). According to Crossick (2016), the monograph allows for the "full examination of a topic . . . woven together in a reflective narrative that is not possible in a journal article" (p. 15).

Annotated Bibliography

While a bibliography is a list of sources used to research a particular topic or phenomenon, an annotated bibliography provides a summary and evaluation of each source (Purdue OWL, 2018e). The annotated bibliography will include a formatted reference, such as those found in a bibliography, followed by an annotation. Annotations are written in paragraph form and include a summary of the main points of the article; an assessment of how the article relates to the topic, phenomenon, or research question; and a reflection of what may be missing from the article and/or if the source is reliable, biased, and what the goal of the article may be (Purdue OWL, 2018a).

Case Study

A case study is an in-depth analysis of real-life events intended to examine individuals, groups, or events in their natural environment (Hancock & Algozzine, 2016). To successfully complete the assignment in criminal justice courses, students are often required to (1) summarize an actual event and identify a problem, (2) provide a detailed explanation of how the problem was addressed or resolved, and (3) critically analyze the resolution by applying course materials, criminal justice theory, and the findings and conclusions of research from previous study of the same or a similar problem.

Legal Analysis

The legal analysis assignment is a research paper in which a student must analyze a set of facts within the context of applicable law. Professors often assign a case study as part of a Constitutional Law, State Law, or Civil Law course. Students are required to research judicial opinions, state statutes and constitutions, the U.S. Constitution, and administrative law (Rowe, 2009). It is particularly important for students to ensure the applied law is not outdated or appealed (Rowe, 2009).

Writing in Corrections

Thinking critically and writing for academic classes is great practice for the profession of criminal justice. Similarly, the criminal justice professions require a variety of written work. Harvey (2015) notes the most powerful instrument a criminal justice officer carries is a pen. These are strong words considering the many weapons carried by criminal justice practitioners. If a report is poorly written, readers are less likely to take the content seriously and may question the writer's credibility, which, in the criminal justice system, can have serious consequences (Harrison, Weisman, & Zornado, 2017). The following is a short list of the legal consequences of poorly written reports:

1. Drug case dismissed and inmates released due to bad search warrant (Astolfi, 2016).
2. Killers go free due to incomplete police reports (Haner, Wilson, & O'Donnell, 2002).
3. Police Credibility on Trial in D.C. Courts

   Drawing the jury's attention to such a discrepancy—by having an officer read aloud from his arrest report—gives a defense lawyer an opening to explore whether the officer might have been wrong about other important facts (Flaherty & Harriston, 1994).
4. Words Used in Sexual Assault Reports Can Hurt Cases

   Poorly written reports—sometimes laden with implications of disbelief or skepticism—can contaminate a jury's perception of a victim's credibility or cripple a case altogether (Dissell, 2010).
5. Officers Indicted by Federal Grand Jury

   Three Georgia officers charged with writing false reports to cover up police assault (U.S. Department of Justice, 2014).

Policing Reports

While this text focuses on writing in corrections, it is important for correctional officers to be aware of several different types of police reports as well. Police officers are required to write a narrative in many different types of documents. Many agencies use a cover page of check boxes and blank spaces to indicate the type of incident being documented, demographic information, and the address of the parties involved. Many of these same documents, though, require the officer to complete a detailed, written narrative that accurately documents the officer's observations and actions, statements made by victims, witnesses, and suspects, any evidence collected, and other information relevant to the case. Policing documents are often written in a narrative format in which the officer tells a story of his or her involvement in an official event.

Most documents used in corrections do not require a written narrative. Many documents can be effectively completed by selecting a check box or entering demographic or descriptive information in a content box.

Field Notes

Field notes are commonly used in policing. Notes taken at a crime scene are vital to the accuracy of initial and follow-up reports. Officers are also able to refer to their field notes to refresh their memory during deposition and trial in most states. Note taking is the process of gathering and recording facts and information relevant to the police investigation. Officers gather a variety of information in a quick and efficient manner so they may recall the facts of the case to write the incident report, assist follow-up investigations, and refresh their memory for court testimony.

Incident Report

Like in policing, corrections officers often find the need to write an incident report. This report can be used to officially document events including criminal activity, violation of institutional policy, discovered contraband, and incidents between officers and inmates, as well as those between inmates. They may also be used to justify inmate discipline, segregation, or use of force by an officer.

Supplemental Report

This report is an addendum to the incident report. The supplemental report is often used by officers and investigators to add information to the incident report. The supplemental report is most often used to document interviews, evidence collected, or other activity related to a case that occurred after an officer's original incident report.

Evidence

The evidence report is used to document any item that has been seized by an officer or has evidentiary value. It also establishes a chain of custody so that seized items can be presented in court. Advances in the technology available to criminal justice agencies have expanded the scope of items of evidentiary value to include video and audio recorded on cell phones, body and in-car cameras, housing unit cameras located in adult and juvenile detention facilities, courtroom cameras, and surveillance cameras. This report is also an addendum to the incident report.

Grants

Many local criminal justice agencies struggle to continue to offer a level of service enjoyed in the past as revenues shrink and budgets are dramatically reduced. There will always be crime, but criminal justice professionals and professors alike are often forced to find new funding sources to create or test new ideas and programs (Davis, 1999).

Perhaps not often enough, these agencies seek out grant funding to supplement personnel and equipment costs, finance community service programs, and fund new initiatives that otherwise would not be possible. According to Karsh and Fox (2014), a grant "is an award of money that allows you to do very specific things that usually meet very specific guidelines that are spelled out in painstaking detail and to which you must respond very clearly in your grant proposal" (p. 12). The field of criminal justice—academically and professionally—has benefited greatly from grant funding (Davis, 1999).

Grant funds can come from a number of sources, including the federal government, corporations, foundations, and even individuals. The federal government, through Grants.gov, is the most prominent grant provider for criminal justice agencies. The U.S. Department of Justice (DOJ) offers grant funding to local and state law enforcement agencies to "assist victims of crime; to provide training and technical assistance; to conduct research; and to implement programs that improve the criminal, civil, and juvenile justice systems" (DOJ, 2018). Through the Office of Community Oriented Policing, the Office of Justice Systems, and the Office of Violence Against Women, the DOJ provides grants to support the hiring and training of police officers, implementation of crime control programs, and reduction of violence against women (DOJ, 2018). Similarly, the Bureau of Justice Assistance provides grant funding for "law enforcement, prosecution, indigent defense, courts, crime prevention and education, corrections and community corrections, [and] drug treatment" (Office of Justice Programs, 2018). Criminal justice agencies can also establish partnerships with academic institutions. According to Gerardi and Wolff (2008), one such collaborative effort yielded over $6 million to a corrections institution over a 5-year period.

CHAPTER SUMMARY

Writing well is an important skill for criminal justice students and professionals. Academic writing assignments improve the student's research, credibility, and writing skills in preparation for future criminal justice careers. Poor writing can discredit a student, officer, and/or criminal justice agency's reputation.

Common writing assignments for criminal justice students include essays, case studies, annotated bibliographies, and legal analysis. In addition to gaining a deeper understanding of criminal justice topics and current issues, assignments such as these enhance critical thinking, an essential skill in the criminal justice professions since it is a key piece of problem solving.

Corrections professionals are required to write a variety of report narratives, such as an incident report or grant. As Harrison, Weisman, and Zornado (2017) aptly note, a poorly written report may bring into question the writer's credibility, which, in the criminal justice system, can have serious consequences.

ADDITIONAL READING

Strunk, W. (2011). *The elements of style*. Project Gutenberg. Retrieved from https://www.gutenberg.org/files/37134/37134-h/37134-h.htm

Purdue Online Writing Lab. (2018). General writing resources. Retrieved from https://owl.english.purdue.edu/owl/section/1/

QUESTIONS FOR CONSIDERATION

1. Why is writing well important in corrections?
2. What functions does the basic incident report serve?
3. Who might read an incident report inside the corrections agency? Outside the agency?
4. Define critical thinking. How is critical thinking important to criminal justice students and practitioners?
5. List three documents commonly used in corrections agencies. Describe how these documents are used and why they are important.

EXERCISE ANSWERS

Exercise 1.1 Answers

1. inmate (subject) entered (verb).
2. inmate (subject) smashed (verb).
3. He (subject) removed (verb).
4. stereo (subject) is valued (verb).
5. I (subject) processed (verb).
6. inmate (subject) punched (verb).
7. inmate (subject) removed (verb).
8. I (subject) responded (verb).
9. I (subject) moved (verb).
10. I (subject) transported (verb).

Exercise 1.2 Answers

1. We approached the defendant, and Corrections Officer Smith asked to buy a "dime."
2. We approached the defendant and asked to buy a "dime."
3. At today's Day-Shift briefing, Sgt. Jones asked for volunteers.
4. I charged the defendant with sale and delivery of cocaine, possession of cocaine, and possession of drug paraphernalia.
5. Sgt. Jones, the Day-Shift supervisor, asked for volunteers.
6. I arrested the defendant for shoplifting, yet he denied the charge.
7. I am usually assigned to Pod D, but today I am working in Pod A.
8. Today I wrote reports for burglary, theft, and battery.
9. Corrections Officer, an experienced drug agent, made a cocaine seizure today.

Exercise 1.3 Answers

1. We responded to the call; Corrections Officer wrote the report.
2. At briefing the sergeant asked for volunteers and reports.
3. I saw the nurse treating the victim; she had a stomach wound.
4. The defendant removed the item from the shelf; she then left the store after failing to pay.
5. I am assigned to Pod C; I primarily work the recreation yard.

Exercise 1.4 Answers

1. I charged the inmate with the following: assault, battery, and theft.
2. The following attachments are provided with this report: sworn statements, and evidence form.
3. I testified on several cases today while in court: 92-123456, 90-123456, and 89-123456.

Exercise 1.5 Answers

1. The victim said, "He stabbed me in the stomach."
2. "He stabbed me in the stomach," she said.
3. She said, "He stabbed me in the stomach"; but I saw no wound.
4. The officer asked, "Who attacked you?"
5. Who was it who said "Live and let live"?

Exercise 1.6 Answers

1. its
2. it's
3. there
4. there
5. their
6. they're, there
7. lie
8. laid, lie
9. who
10. whom
11. who

CHAPTER 2

What Is Information Literacy?

The average person is bombarded with the equivalent of 174 newspapers of data each day (Alleyne, 2011). The Internet, television, and mobile phones have increased the amount of information a person receives by five times as compared to 1986 (Alleyne, 2011). According to researchers at the University of Southern California, the digital age allows people to send out more information by email, Twitter, social networking sites, and text messages than at any other time in history. In 1986, each individual generated approximately two and half pages of information a day; however, in 2007, each person produced the equivalent of six 85-page newspapers daily (Hilbert & Lopez, 2011). Imagine how that may have changed in the last decade! As one can guess, all of this information has to be stored and catalogued. It also has to be analyzed and sorted using our own interpretations and those presented by the media and other outlets. In a world where fake news and social media dominate most of what people read and hear each day, individuals have to be more savvy and use more critical thinking than ever in distinguishing good information from bad information. Individuals also have to be skilled in acquiring facts and in deciding when information is needed and what to take from the data they gather. In other words, people have to be competent in *information literacy*. In this chapter, information literacy will be defined, and the skills needed to become an information literate person will be identified. Additionally, information literacy and its relationship to technology and critical thinking will be discussed. Examples of how information literacy is used in criminal justice will be provided throughout the chapter.

Information Literacy

Information literacy is not just another buzzword. It is a skill that people can develop over time with the proper understanding of research, analysis, and writing. Information literacy is a crucial talent in the pursuit of knowledge, and it is required in the professional world. It is important in workforces that require lifelong learning, like criminal justice, and it is seen as a linking pin to economic development in education, business, and government (National Forum on Information Literacy, 2018). The National Forum on Information Literacy (2018, para. 3), sponsored by the American Library Association, defined information literacy as a person's ability to "know when they need information, to identify information that can help them address the issue or problem at hand, and to locate, evaluate, and use that information effectively." Most colleges and universities recognize that students should be informationally literate when they graduate. In fact, in 2000, the Association of Colleges and Research Libraries developed the Information Literacy Competency Standards for Higher Education, and in 2004, the American Association for Higher Education and the Council of Independent Colleges endorsed the standards (Stanford's Key to Information Literacy, 2018). Information literacy is considered a key objective for many university and discipline-specific accrediting bodies. Supporting this goal is the belief that information literacy is linked to critical thinking (another objective commanded by colleges and accrediting agencies) because the two skills appear to share very common objectives (Breivik, 2005).

Like information literacy, critical thinking skills require individuals to explore and evaluate ideas for the purpose of forming opinions, problem-solving, and making decisions (Wertz et al., 2013). It has been argued that in both critical thinking and information literacy, individuals must collect information and evaluate its quality and relevance. Then, the individuals must integrate the information into their current understandings or belief systems on particular topics. Finally, in both critical thinking and information literacy, individuals must use the information to draw conclusions and understand the limitations of the information on those conclusions (Wertz et al., 2013). According to Wertz et al. (2013), doing all of this allows for effective decision making.

Other researchers, like Breivik (2005), have argued that it requires critical thinking skills to be information literate because individuals need to analytically assess the information overload they encounter when using technology. Further, a study of digital classrooms in Hong Kong (Kong, 2014) found that using digital classrooms to enhance domain knowledge also increased critical thinking skills among secondary students in a 13-week trial period. However, not all researchers are convinced there is a direct correlation between information literacy and critical thinking. Ward (2006) argued that information literacy goes beyond critical thinking by forcing individuals to manage information in creative and meaningful ways, not to just analyze it. Albtiz (2007) claimed that information literacy is skill based, while critical thinking requires higher order cognitive processes. Finally, Wieler (2005) stated that students in the early years of college may be able to find and access information but may not yet have the ability to critically analyze it because they have not developed beyond a dualistic intellectual capacity. Thus, even though students may find the information needed, they may wait for an authority figure, like a professor, to tell them the answer to the problem. The actual relationship between information literacy and critical thinking skills may well be a chicken-and-egg argument wherein the question is if a person needs critical thinking skills to develop information literacy or if information literacy can increase critical thinking skills. It is likely that the two are intertwined. Regardless of the answer to this question, there appears to be enough evidence to convince universities and accrediting bodies that both skills are absolutely required to produce effective, productive, and successful students and employees.

Just like students are expected to use critical thinking in their academic work, information literacy is common today in all academic disciplines and

Figure 2.1 Information Literacy

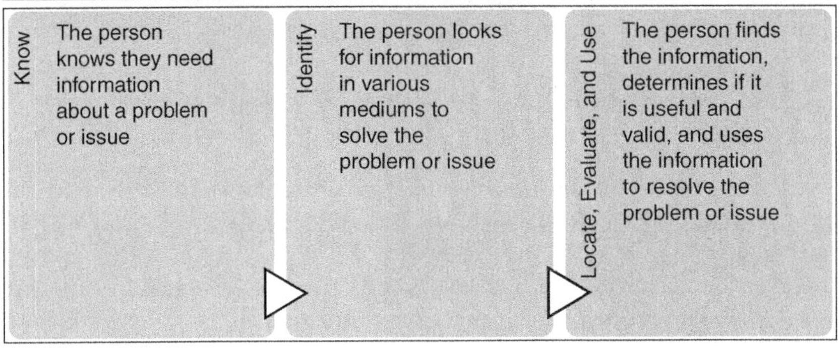

is used in all learning environments. Many times, students are exposed to activities in classrooms that are designed to build skills in information literacy without even realizing it. Most students in college have probably used information literacy to write a research paper or to respond to a class assignment. But gathering information on a single topic does not just stop there. The information has to be analyzed for usefulness and presented in a way that solves a problem or provides more focus to an issue. Information literacy requires that a person also uses the information gathered in ethical and legal ways and that he or she assumes greater control over the investigation and becomes more self-directed in the pursuit of knowledge (Association of College and Research Libraries, 2000). In fact, the Information Literacy Competency Standards for Higher Education require that an information literate person

1. Determine the extent of information needed
2. Access the needed information effectively and efficiently
3. Evaluate information and its sources critically
4. Incorporate selected information into one's knowledge base
5. Use information effectively to accomplish a specific purpose
6. Understand the economic, legal, and social issues surrounding the use of information, and access and use information ethically and legally (Association of College and Research Libraries, 2000, pp. 2–3)

Information literacy is related to information technology skills and extends beyond reading a book or listening to the news. Information literacy includes the technology-enriched digital information world. People use *digital literacy skills* when they rely on technology to communicate with family and friends; *computer literacy skills* when they use hardware, software, peripherals, and network components; and *technology literacy* to work independently and with others to effectively use electronic tools to access, manage, integrate, evaluate, create, and communicate information (Stanford's Key to Information Literacy, 2018). Each of these skills is interwoven with and overlaps the broader concept of information literacy, as information literate individuals will inevitably develop skills in technology during their pursuit of information.

Using Information Literacy—Know, Identify, Evaluate, and Use

As suggested by the Information Literacy Competency Standards for Higher Education (Association of College and Research Libraries, 2000), information literate individuals will follow a process in identifying and using information to resolve problems or issues. This process requires the person to know, identify, evaluate, and use information effectively, ethically, and legally. This process is summarized in the paragraphs that follow.

Know of a Problem or Issue That Needs to Be Resolved

A person may become aware of a problem or issue in a variety of ways. The person may experience a situation that bothers him or her and makes the individual want to resolve it so no one else experiences the same situation. Consider the case of Megan Kanka, who was kidnapped, sexually assaulted, and murdered by a man who had two previous convictions for sexual offenses. He moved into a home directly across the street from Megan prior to the crime. Neither Megan's parents nor their neighbors knew of his background. After her murder and the efforts of her parents to prevent similar crimes in other areas, Megan's Law was passed. Megan's Law created a sex offender notification system, which provides information on sex offenders to communities when a potentially dangerous sex offender moves into the neighborhood (Larson, 2016). Every state now tracks sex offenders and provides information to the public on them.

A person may be told that there is a problem or issue—perhaps through a meeting (e.g., inmates are complaining about an increased number of bugs in the cells), by constituents (e.g., a citizen writes a letter to the mayor complaining that inmates are cleaning the community center while children are present), on the news or through social media (e.g., a friend posts a video of a correctional officer abusing an inmate on Facebook), or by noticing a pattern in data (e.g., court statistics show increases in minority incarceration rates). A student, for example, may be told to complete an assignment by a teacher that seeks to solve a problem or make recommendations about a social issue, like child abuse. Knowing about the problem or issue allows for the process of information literacy to start.

Identify Information

Once a person is aware that there is a problem or issue that he or she needs to resolve, the individual will begin the information gathering process. There are a couple of avenues a person may choose to gather information. He or she may use an information retrieval system, like the library or a database. A probation officer, for example, may identify a high number of homeless offenders by using case data on parolees. Another option is for a person to use lab-based activities or simulations to gather information. For example, to identify weaknesses in the institution's perimeter, a correctional facility may hold mock emergency scenarios that replicate riots or a prison escapes. A third approach may be for the person to use an investigative technique, like surveys or interviews. For example, a corrections officer may discuss concerns about food, safety, or housing with inmates. Once the officer learns that inmates feel unsafe because of increased gang activity or overcrowding, the officer can decide what to do with the remarks. Physical examination can also be used to gather information. Viewing and photographing a crime scene firsthand or witnessing an event with your own eyes can provide a wealth of information about an issue or problem. As an example, an imate may report on increased officer harassment during the evening shift at the prison. Rather than taking the inmate's word, a warden may have shift supervisors watch security cameras for officer activity and/or work in each unit during the shift, so they can witness the officer-inmate interactions for themselves. Witnessing the interactions provides the information needed for the warden to evaluate and determine the best course of action for the criminal activity.

Evaluate the Information

The person who is adept at information literacy will find the information he or she is looking for using various mediums, as discussed above. Then, the person will evaluate the abundant pieces of information found. In the evaluation process, the person is tasked with trying to determine whether the information is valid and reliable. The sources of the information should be examined critically to determine if the source is credible. To do this, the Centers for Disease Control and Prevention (n.d.) suggests that the information literate person assess the information by asking several questions:

1. **Where did the information come from?** This consideration is focused exclusively on the source of the information. In the case of information retrieval systems, the person may assess the journal article and the journal in which the article was published. The information literate person may read the introduction of the journal to determine if the journal is scientific and if the article was peer reviewed. Knowing that an article that undergoes peer review is much more reliable than an article published in a magazine allows the information literate person to accept the information in the article as trustworthy. Using an example from above, the probation officer who evaluates parolee case data and who is familiar with the validity and reliability of these data can make a logical and well-informed decision about how best to handle the increasing number of homeless parolees.
2. **How does the new information fit with what is already known about the problem or issue?** The corrections officer who discussed issues and concerns with inmates may want to compare these complaints with menus in the cafeteria, inmate daily population statistics as related to housing, and inmate characteristics and affiliations. He may also want to talk to other

corrections officers who work with inmates to see if they are noticing increasing conflicts among inmates or issues with space and meals. Comparing the various pieces of information to one another and to information that was gathered previously allows the individual to determine which pieces of data to keep and which to discard. If the officer has worked as a corrections officer for a while, he may already know where the issues lie.

3. **Is funding involved in the creation of the information?** Although funding may not be a part of every equation in solving an issue or problem, the ability to report findings in a study without bias can be skewed if the researcher writing the report has been funded by an outside source. In other words, the source of the funding for a research project may bias the reporting of the results. If funding is present, the source (e.g., journal article, news report) should include that information. When reading an article or listening to a report, the information literate person needs to consider if the funders had anything to gain by the results. If so, questions of validity and credibility in the findings may exist. Consider the findings of a study on a youth mentoring program where the employees of the program completed the data analysis and where the study was paid for using program funds. If the study results demonstrated that the program was not working, the program may be closed, and the employees would need to find another job. If the funders did not have a stake in the results of the study, the funding will likely have less influenced the findings. A person evaluating the information for legitimacy should always contemplate the existence of funding.

4. **Can you trust the information from television, magazines, the Internet, and brochures?** Some reports in the media are based on peer-reviewed journal articles but some are not. Again, when hearing a report, one has to question where the information came from—the source—not who is reporting the information. Accordingly, a person should not just believe ABC News when they report record numbers in parole violations; instead, the individual should listen for the source of ABC News' information, which is hopefully the Federal Bureau of Prisons. The information literate person should also question if the information is consistent with previous information. For example, the media may claim that a finding is conclusive even though a single study's findings are never considered irrefutable, and other media outlets may be providing information in contrary to the news story. The information literate person must recognize that news stories focus on what is "new" and "exciting." Television stations need to sell advertising space to stay in business, and advertisers want to buy advertising space on television stations with the most number of viewers. The same goes for magazines and businesses that produce brochures. Funding may play a key role in the types of stories reported and/or the focus of the stories.

Thanks to President Trump, few people are not aware of the term *fake news*. Fake news seems to be all the buzz these days. Although it may not

Exercise 2.1

You are a probation officer. You receive a call about a probationer being involved in a domestic disturbance at a home on the south side of town. As you arrive at the home, you see two adults and four children standing in the yard. There are also three neighbors standing in the street. You know that you must use information literacy skills to determine what to do in the current situation. Using each of the skills identified in the chapter—know there is a problem, locate information, evaluate information, use and share the information—explain what steps you will take to resolve the domestic issue and the probation violation that may have occurred.

be a new trend, it has historically been used in news satire, the fact that the information shared in fake news is widely accepted as a reality is concerning. Fake news articles exist on television, in magazines, and most popularly, on social media and the Internet. Fake news can include completely made-up stories that resemble credible journalism; stories that are only a little bit fake, such as stories that report actual truth but use distorted or decontextualized headlines to convince people to click on their web links; and news stories that are satirical or sarcastic (Hunt, 2016). Often times, the goal behind fake news on the Internet is to entice a reader to click on the story and visit a website to gain advertising revenue for the person hosting the website. According to a report in the *Guardian*, a man who was running a fake news website in Los Angeles told National Public Radio that he has made as much as $30,000 a month from advertising that rewards high traffic to his website (Hunt, 2016). Identifying fake news can be rather difficult, especially in criminal justice; however, the In the News 2.1 shows an example of fake

In the News 2.1

Thousands of Fake Ballot Slips Found Marked for Hillary Clinton

http://yournewswire.com/thousands-ballot-slips-hillary-clinton/
October 1, 2016, by Baxter Dmitry

Reports are emerging that "tens of thousands" of fraudulent ballot slips have been found in a downtown Columbus, Ohio, warehouse, and the votes are all pre-marked for Hillary Clinton and other Democratic Party candidates.

Randall Prince, a Columbus-area electrical worker, was performing routine checks of his companies wiring and electrical systems when he stumbled across approximately one dozen black, sealed ballot boxes filled with thousands of Franklin County votes for Hillary Clinton and other Democratic Party candidates.

"No one really goes in this building. It's mainly used for short-term storage by a commercial plumber," Prince said.

So when Prince, a Trump supporter, saw several black boxes in an otherwise empty room, he went to investigate. What he found could be evidence of an alleged election fraud operation designed to deliver Clinton the crucial swing state.

Early voting does not begin in Ohio until October 12, so no votes have officially been cast in the Buckeye state. However, inside these boxes were, what one source described as, "potentially tens of thousands of votes" for Hillary Clinton.

An affiliate in Ohio passed along a replica of the documents found in the boxes:

(*Continued*)

(Continued)

OFFICIAL GENERAL ELECTION BALLOT

COLS 14-E 01

A	Franklin County, Ohio	B	General Election	C	November 8, 2016

Instructions to Voter

- **To vote:** completely darken the oval (⬬) to the left of your choice.
- Note the permitted number of choices directly below the title of each candidate office. Do not mark the ballot for more choices than allowed. Vote either "Yes" or "No," or "For" or "Against," on any issue.
- If you mark the ballot for more choices than permitted, that contest or question will not be counted.
- **To vote for a write-in candidate:** completely darken the oval (⬬) to the left of the blank line and write in the candidate's name. Only votes cast for candidates who filed as write-in candidates can be counted.
- Do not write in a candidate's name if that person's name is already printed on the ballot for that same contest.
- **If you make a mistake or want to change your vote:** return your ballot to an election official and get a new ballot. You may ask for a new ballot up to two times.

For President and Vice President
(Vote for not more than 1 pair)
A vote for any candidates for President and Vice President shall be a vote for the electors of those candidates whose names have been certified to the Secretary of State.

- For President **Jill Stein** For Vice President **Ajamu Baraka** Green
- For President **Donald J. Trump** For Vice President **Michael R. Pence** Republican
- For President **Hillary Clinton** For Vice President **Tim Kaine** Democratic
- For President **Richard Duncan** For Vice President **Ricky Johnson** Nonparty Candidates

For U.S. Senator
(Vote for not more than 1)

- **Scott Rupert** Nonparty Candidate
- **Ted Strickland** Democratic
- **Tom Connors** Nonparty Candidate
- **Joseph R. DeMare** Green
- **Rob Portman** Republican
- Write-In

For Representative to Congress (15th District)
(Vote for not more than 1)

- **Scott Wharton** Democratic
- **Steve Stivers** Republican

For State Representative (18th District)
(Vote for not more than 1)

- **Kristin Boggs**

For Prosecuting Attorney
(Vote for not more than 1)

- **Bob Fitrakis** Green
- **Zach Klein** Democratic
- **Ron O'Brien** Republican

For Clerk of the Court of Common Pleas
(Vote for not more than 1)

- **Maryellen O'Shaughnessy** Democratic
- **Besa Sharrah** Republican

For Sheriff
(Vote for not more than 1)

- **Dallas L. Baldwin** Democratic

For County Recorder
(Vote for not more than 1)

- **Daphne Hawk** Republican
- **Danny O'Connor** Democratic

For County Treasurer
(Vote for not more than 1)

- **Ted A. Berry** Republican

It is important to note that the above replica coincides with a ballot that a Franklin County voter would cast at the polling place on Election Day, meaning the Clinton campaign's likely goal was to slip the fake ballot boxes in with the real ballot boxes when they went to official election judges on November 8th.

Ohio, a perennial swing state in the presidential election, has been a challenge for Clinton and her Democrat counterparts in 2016. Many national Democrat groups have pulled funding from the state entirely, in order to redirect it to places in which they are doing better.

Clinton herself has spent less time in Ohio, and spent less money, in recent weeks as it has appeared that Trump will carry the crucial state.

With this find, however, it now appears that Clinton and the Democrat Party planned on stealing the state on Election Day, making any campaigning there now a waste of time.

This story is still developing, and more news will be published when we have it.

news involving political fraud. The story was published on the Internet and spread through social media, reaching over 6.1 million people before it was discredited by Snopes.com (Garcia & Lear, 2016).

Spotting fake news and evaluating it is not easy because society is flooded with news stories all day, every day. Taking the time to assess and evaluate each one may be an impossibility. However, the information literate individual can rely on the skills he or she has learned to evaluate information to spot fake news. He or she can also look for fake news indicators, such as websites with red flags in their names like ".com.co" and by looking at a website's "About Us" page to determine the website's sources. The individual can use Google Chrome plugins to filter fake news articles from their Internet searches and can google the sources of any quotes or figures in articles he or she may read on the Internet or on social media. Additionally, the information literate person should question websites that he or she has never heard of before. Obscure websites or websites that end in ".org" may have an agenda behind their reporting practices (Hung, 2016). Finally, using websites to fact check an article, like Snopes.com, which is a fact-checking website with more than 20 years of information, may help to evaluate the credibility of the information provided.

The authors of this book would be remiss if we did not mention that students should be cautious when using the Internet for research and information gathering in the first place. Libraries, both electronic and brick-and-mortar, are still the best and most consistent places to find legitimate information. Even though the Internet provides a plethora of information, not all of it is reliable. Anyone can publish anything he or she wants (as long as it is not illegal) on the Internet, even going so far as to make the website where the information published looks genuine. Unlike journal articles that may undergo peer review, websites are not monitored for quality, accuracy, or bias. A popular example of this is Wikipedia.org. Students often refer to and cite Wikipedia in research papers, and Wikipedia claims to be an encyclopedia. Yet Wikipedia is an information website with "openly editable content" (Wikipedia: About, 2018, para. 1). Anyone with access to the Internet can modify a page on the Wikipedia.com website, and anonymous contributors edit most of the content on the website. Although Wikipedia.org contends that the information contributed must be verifiable and come from a reliable source, anyone can post information on Wikipedia.org about a topic whether he or she knows anything about the topic or not (Wikipedia: About, 2018, para. 4). Thus, it is especially important that the information literate person evaluate or use critical thinking skills to assess the resource closely on Wikipedia and all other websites.

When evaluating websites, individuals should consider whether the name of the author or creator of the information is published on the website. He or she should also consider the author or creator's credentials. Asking questions about the author or creator's occupation and experience with the subject matter, position, or education is crucial. Additionally, the information literate person should determine if the author is qualified to write about the topic and if there is contact information for the author or creator somewhere on the website. Another factor to consider is if the author or creator is writing for or associated with an organization. In other words, could their role in the organization potentially influence what is published on the website? The reader may also want to take into account the URL identification and domain name. Domain names with ".org" indicate an affiliation with an organization, while ".com" and ".biz" may be commercial or for-profit websites. Domain names like ".edu" and ".gov" commonly publish articles that have undergone review and may be scientific in nature, although it is still the reader's responsibility to determine their legitimacy by considering the other features of the website.

Although using a search engine, like Google, Yahoo, Bing, or Ask, is a simple way to find websites and articles on a topic, the information literate person has to comb through the web links provided using the factors discussed above to identify those that are most beneficial and valid. Aside from the random Internet websites that may appear in a web search, there are collections of works on search engines, like Google Scholar, where the information literate person can identify scholarly articles from a number of disciplines. Most of the articles on Google Scholar are peer reviewed and provide the author's name, citation, and location where the article is published. Google Scholar regularly provides links to libraries or websites on the Internet where students can find additional scholarly articles on the topic. Regardless of the type of Internet resource an information literate person chooses to use, asking questions about the purpose, objectivity, accuracy, reliability, credibility, and currency of each website is key to identifying appropriate information (Georgetown University Library, 2018).

Finally, it is during the evaluation process that information is deemed relevant, not relevant, or invalid. This is where critical thinking skills are most important, as the individual analyzes and assesses each piece of information. Relevant information is kept for future use while the information literate person dismisses information considered not relevant or invalid. The person then moves into the final phase of the process—*using the information effectively, ethically, and legally.*

Uses the Information Effectively, Ethically, and Legally

Once the information literate person identifies the new information, he or she will consider it in combination with prior information and use all of the information to effectively resolve a problem or issue. In using the information, the individual will organize the information and present it in a way that provides a resolution to the problem or issue. The information literate person may write a paper or proposal or do a presentation to an interested audience. The information literate person may also create or implement policy or use the information for their personal lifestyle or work changes. In whatever way the individual uses the information, he or she should strive to share it with an audience through technology or personal communication.

The information acquired should also be used ethically and legally. This requires the information literate person to understand the ethical, legal, and socioeconomic issues involved with the information and the medium in which it is shared. Issues such as privacy and security in printing, posting, or broadcasting should be considered. The individual should also consider censorship and freedom of speech issues as well as copyright and fair use laws (Association of College and Research Libraries, 2000).

Copyright laws protect original works of authorship to include literary, dramatic, musical, and artistic works, as well as computer software and architecture. Copyright laws do not protect ideas, facts, systems, or methods of operations; however, the way these are extracted may be protected (U.S. Copyright Office, n.d.). To ethically use information and under copyright laws, individuals are required to provide credit to the original authors of works when using a protected work. If they do not and the originator finds out, he or she can sue the person who used the work without credit or permission. Fair use laws are a clause in the copyright laws that allow non-profit and educational institutions and libraries to reproduce works from original authors, prepare derivative works from the original works, and distribute copies of original works by sale or lease or other means. These entities can also perform the work publicly to include digital audio transmission and to display the copyrighted work (U.S. Copyright Office, n.d.). Although specific guidelines are attached to fair use, like the inability to photocopy textbooks or distribute copyrighted information to others, providing commentary, criticism, news reporting, and using copyrighted material in research and scholarship are allowable (when credit is provided to the original author). Individuals can also ethically and legally use information in the public domain. Although many believe that all of the information found on the Internet is public domain, this is not true. Works that fall within the public domain include those in which the intellectual property rights have expired, been forfeited, been waived, or where they do not apply. U.S. government documents are excluded from copyright law and are considered as public domain. All other works, even those found on the Internet, are the intellectual property of the person who created them and fall within copyright-protected statutes. Information literate individuals must be diligent in their understanding of how information falls within copyright, fair use, and public domain regulations. These parameters are country based and can vary—meaning what is copyrighted in one country may be public domain in another (U.S. Copyright Office, n.d.). As such, providing credit to the originator or gaining permission to use the work is always the safest approach. The Digital Copyright Slider (2012) created by Michael Brewer and the American Library Association Office for Information Technology Policy is a practical guide for determining copyright, fair use, and public domain.

Developing information literacy skills takes time and effort. Information literate individuals practice the skills by becoming better and more efficient at locating, analyzing, and using the information. Often this practice requires the person to use technology in the process. Thus, he or she develops digital literacy, computer literacy, and technology literacy skills in addition to information literacy skills.

Digital Literacy, Computer Literacy, and Technology Literacy Skills

The information literate person will develop digital, computer, and technology literacy skills as he or she investigates topics using information literacy. These skills will likely become more effective over time and will greatly assist in gathering and dispersing information. Developing these skills allows collaboration with individuals near and far and dissemination of information beyond the intended audiences. As such, these skills, like being information literate, should be used within ethical and legal guidelines, namely privacy, copyright, confidentiality, and authorship.

Digital literacy is the "ability to use information and communication technologies to find, evaluate, create, and communicate information, requiring both cognitive and technical skills" (American Library Association, 2018, para. 2). Digital literacy includes reading digital content and using digital formats to find and create content. For example, reading a book on a Kindle is digital literacy, as is using a search engine to find articles on sex offender treatment programs and sharing the results of a therapy session video with friends and family on social media. Another example is sending an email or tweeting about a weekend activity.

Digital literacy includes digital writing, which may involve emailing, blogging, tweeting, and so on. Digital writing is intended to be shared with others, so understanding its role in the social, legal, and economic community is important. Digital writing can be a potentially precarious tool if the information literate person does not consider the privacy implications of what he or she creates and shares and/or the safety and legal implications of sharing the information (Heitin, 2016). Consider an example where a 13-year-old girl takes a picture of her genitals and Snapchats it to a boyfriend. If the boyfriend saves the photo and sends it to other friends, he may face criminal charges for distributing child pornography. By receiving the picture, he may also face criminal charges if he fails to report the photo to the proper adult or authority. The girl may face criminal charges for distributing child pornography. In this scenario, the picture may travel phone-to-phone through many youth, each facing their own privacy and legal issues when they receive, open, view, and, possibly, share the photo. The moral here is there is an increased responsibility that comes with digital writing and literacy that may not be as pressing in print writing. Print writing, depending on the source, customarily undergoes review before being disseminated, whereas digital information may not.

Computer literacy means that an individual has the basic knowledge and skills to use a computer. The person may be familiar with turning the computer on and off, word processing, printing documents, and so on. As the individual uses the computer, he or she may become even more literate in using other types of programs, operating systems, software applications, and web design. Computer literacy

> can be understood in the same way that traditional literacy applies to print media. However, because computers are much more advanced than print media in terms of access, operation and overall use, computer literacy includes many more types of cognitive and technical skills, from understanding text and visual symbols, to turning devices on and off or accessing parts of an operating system through menus. (technopedia.com, 2018, para. 2)

Being able to code, develop web pages, and network administration are higher level skills developed by some computer literate individuals. Although not everyone will develop computer literacy skills comparable to a technical support assistant, most information literate individuals develop enough skills to surf the web, identify sources, develop documents and presentations, and disseminate information through the appropriate computer venues. For example, a corrections officer presenting training on prison paraphernalia may develop a PowerPoint presentation. A web technician employed by a state department of corrections to maintain the department's website may post updated incarceration statistics, mission statements, and pictures of corrections officers working in the prison.

Exercise 2.2

What ethical issues might an individual who posts information on social media face? What about legal issues? Provide an example post from a social media website and discuss both the ethical and legal issues.

There are individuals who develop computer literacy skills but use them for illegal activity. They may create viruses, hack websites, and send out bogus or scam emails. The AARP reported in a survey of more than 11,000 Internet users that two-thirds received spam emails at least once per year (Paulas, 2016). Less computer literate individuals may fall prey to these phishing emails, especially if the emails closely mimic bank websites or formal notices from other businesses. Although the police and other social service agencies provide notices when illegal computer activity is flourishing in a specific geographical location, they cannot protect everyone from unethical computer practices. Classes designed to train people in computer literacy can be used to lower the potential for computer victimization, but these often require having discretionary money to pay for the classes. This is something some individuals may not find affordable. The information and computer literate individual will learn over time how to identify and avoid harmful computer practices and will observe legal standards when using the computer.

Quite simply, technology literacy is the ability to use the appropriate technology to communicate and search for information. In technology literacy, a person knows when to use the Internet versus email or when to create a webpage versus a PowerPoint presentation. A prison population analyst, for example, would know when to use an Excel spreadsheet to disseminate inmate population statistics instead of using SPSS, a statistical analysis software package. Developing technology literacy skills is an ongoing process, as instructional and communications technologies change with every new invention. Computers and email are just the tip of the iceberg, as there now exist digitized kitchen appliances, self-driving vehicles, and integrated manufacturing. Who knows what the future holds with regard to technology? Regardless, most agree that technology literacy incorporates four basic skills: (1) the ability to adapt to rapid and continuous technology change; (2) the ability to develop creative solutions to technological problems; (3) the ability to process technological knowledge effectively, efficiently, and ethically; and (4) the ability to assess technology's place in social, cultural, economic, and legal environments (Wonacott, 2001). Developing and using these skills in conjunction with information literacy is vital to identifying information and using it to solve problems. It is also essential to workplace productivity, decision making, global integration, and, on a more micro level, to finding and keeping a job.

In summary, the information literate person who develops digital, computer, and technology literacy is more likely to continue learning and developing new and better critical thinking skills. Additionally, he or she is likely to display other skills desired in the workplace, such as evaluation, analytical thinking, creativity, problem-solving, and research analysis and design skills. The literate person will demonstrate effective skills in decision making, such as acting in moral and ethical ways, and exercise more autonomy and positive work habits (Wonacott, 2001). Each of these skills is essential in the field of criminal justice.

CHAPTER SUMMARY

Information literacy is an acquired skill that allows individuals to know that they need information and to locate, evaluate, use, and share information. Information literacy is usually used to solve problems. Information literate individuals may use a variety of methods to find information, including media, print, the Internet, and other forms of technology. When doing so, the information literate individual is also developing skills in digital, computer, and technology literacy. All forms of literacy discussed in this chapter should be used within ethical and legal considerations. Knowing how the information a person disseminates can affect the social, cultural, economic, and legal environments is especially important in a global society. Information literate individuals have better chances to acquire and keep jobs. They are more likely to display the types of skills employers demand to include critical thinking, evaluation, creativity, higher morals and ethics, and problem-solving abilities, among others. Workplace productivity can be greatly improved when organizations hire information literate persons. In criminal justice, being able to acquire, evaluate, use, and share information is an essential skill applied in every position and in all cases and interactions. When criminal justice professionals are not adept at information literacy, they can ruin cases, cause appeals, and, in general, prevent the system from functioning effectively.

QUESTIONS FOR CONSIDERATION

1. How might a probation officer use technology literacy to do his or her job?
2. Your college professor assigns you a paper for a class project. Using information, digital, computer, and technology literacy, explain how you would complete the project.
3. What confidentiality issues would a parole officer face in gathering and sharing information about parolees?
4. Identify how an information literate person may know a problem or issue exists. What types of sources should he or she disregard when researching problems or issues?

CHAPTER 3

Reports From Pretrial, Probation, and Parole Officers

Within the criminal justice system, there are several officers that work with defendants and offenders to ensure justice is fairly administered. These include pretrial, probation, and parole officers. Pretrial officers work with individuals who are charged with crimes but are awaiting trial. Probation officers work with offenders postconviction (U.S. Courts, n.d.), but prior to a period of incarceration. Parole officers monitor offenders after being released from incarceration. Both pretrial and probation officers investigate for the court and write reports that assist in determining release strategies and the best sentences for offenders (U.S. Courts, n.d.). Probation and parole officers supervise offenders and record their actions on contact sheets. These officers also report to the court when offenders violate the conditions of release. The various reports written by these officers are called *pretrial reports, presentence investigations, contact sheets,* and *revocation petitions.* This chapter will discuss these documents.

Pretrial Reports

Court systems utilize pretrial services to assist in determining if defendants should be released prior to trial. They also use these services to help monitor individuals who are in the community awaiting court dates. Currently, several states and the federal government employ pretrial service officers and view participation in the pretrial system as voluntary on behalf of the defendant. Table 3.1 identifies the usefulness of pretrial service programs according to the U.S. Department of Justice (2001).

Pretrial officers are hired by the court system to investigate persons charged with crimes. Their investigations are designed to verify information known about the individual and to ensure that, if released before trial, the individual will not commit an additional crime before their court date. The reports written by pretrial officers are provided to the court and include information about the person's work, school or military records, family, friends, criminal history and current charge, among other information (U.S. Courts, n.d.). Once a defendant consents to participating in the pretrial process, pretrial officers write the report under the presumption of innocence and interview the accused person to obtain most of the information for the report. The pretrial officer will also interview other individuals, such as supervisors, family members, friends, co-defendants, to name a few, to verify information needed for the report. Even though the officer will work with the defendant

Table 3.1 Key Points of Pretrial Services

- Pretrial services programs perform two crucial functions:
  - Gathering and presenting information about newly arrested defendants and about available release options for use by a judicial officer in making decisions concerning a defendant's pretrial custody or release status.
  - Supervising defendants who are released from custody during the pretrial period by monitoring their compliance with release conditions and by helping to ensure they appear for scheduled court appearances and that they do not endanger community safety.
- Both functions described above are essential for jurisdictions to achieve the central goal of a fair and effective pretrial release/detention policy, which is to minimize unnecessary detention by releasing as many defendants as possible who are likely to appear for scheduled court dates and who will refrain from criminal behavior before trial.
- The pretrial decision has significant consequences for the community. It affects how limited jail space is allocated and how the risks of nonappearance and pretrial crime by released defendants are managed.
- The decision also has important consequences for defendants. It directly affects their ability to assert their innocence, negotiate a disposition, and mitigate the severity of a sentence.
- Pretrial release/detention policies and decisions have very important implications for society's capacity to achieve the ideal of equal justice under law. By providing judicial officers with essential information for decision making and by helping to supervise released defendants, pretrial services programs help courts reduce discrimination based on wealth and other factors not related to risk of flight or danger to the community. Fair and effective pretrial release policies are an essential component of equal justice.
- As pretrial services programs have evolved since the 1960s, they have increasingly demonstrated their capacity to provide information about defendants and about available supervised release options that is relevant to assessing both the risk of flight and the risk to public safety. In some jurisdictions, programs have also developed a capacity to supervise defendants and to help minimize both types of risk.

Source: U.S. Department of Justice. (2001). Pretrial services programs: Responsibilities and Potential. National Institute of Justice, Issues and Practices. Retrieved from https://www.ncjrs.gov/pdffiles1/nij/181939.pdf.

to create the report, the pretrial officer will not discuss the current charge or legal matters with the defendant.

Risk and Needs Assessments

Most pretrial reports are combined with a numerically scored risk and needs assessment, often the Level of Service Inventory—Revised (LSI-R), which is the most widely researched and used risk/needs assessment in pretrial, probation, and parole, that provides quantitative support for releasing or detaining the defendant. The assumption on these assessments is that the lower the score on the risk and needs assessment, the less likely a defendant will commit a new offense before court and the more likely he or she will attend court when ordered. The risk and needs assessments are also used, in some cases, to determine conditions for release prior to trial. An example risk and needs assessment is provided in Figure 3.1.

Figure 3.1 Sample Risk Assessment for Pretrial Release

NEVADA PRETRIAL RISK ASSESSMENT (NPR)

Name: ______________________________

Assessment Date: ______/________/_________ Case #:____________

Country: __________________ Assessor:_________________

DOB: ______/_______/_________ Gender: _________ Male _________ Female

# of Current Charges: ____________________

Most Serious Charge: ______________________

Initial Total Bail Set: $ ____________________________

Race: _____ Hispanic _____ White _____ Black _____ Asian _____ Nat. Amer. _____ Other _____

Verified Cell Phone #: ____________________

Address: _________________ ______ _____________

Deadly Weapon Charge: ______________ Yes ______________ No

City ______________ State ______________ Zip ______________

SCORING ITEMS SCORE

1. Does the Defendant Have a Pending Case at Booking?
   a. Yes—3 pts. b. No—0 pts. _______
2. Age at First Arrest. First Arrest Date_______/_____/______________
   a. Under age 21 yrs. —2 pts.
   b. 22–35 yrs. —1 pt.
   c. 36 plus. —0 pts.
3. Prior Misdemeanor Arrests. Total # Misd. Arrests: ___________
   Total # Misd. Convict:_________
   a. 2 or less—0 pts.
   b. 3–5—1 pt.
   c. 6 plus—2 pts.
4. Prior Felony Arrests. Total # Felony Arrests: ______ Total # Felony Convict: ______
   a. None or 1—0 pts.
   b. 2–4—1 pt.
   c. 5 plus—2 pts.
5. Prior Arrests—Violence: Total # Arrests______ Total # Convict: ______
   a. None—0 pts.
   b. 1 or more—2 pts.
6. Prior FTAs Past 24 Months. Date of Last FTA Warrant: _____/_____/_________
   a. None—0 pts.
   b. 1 FTA Warrant—1 pt.
   c. 2 or more FTA Warrants—2 pts.

(Continued)

Figure 3.1 (Continued)

7. Employment Status at Arrest. List Employer: ________________________
   a. Employed or Student or Retired—0 pts.
   b. Unemployed—2 pts.

8. Residential Status. Date of Residency: _____/___________
   a. Living in current residence 6 mos. or longer—0 pts.
   b. Not lived in same residence 6 mos. or longer—1 pt.
   c. Homeless—3 pts.

9. Substance Abuse
   a. No evidence of drug abuse/alcoholism—0 pts.
   b. Some evidence – current charge—1pt.
   c. Prior multiple arrests for drug possession/alcohol/drunkenness—2 pts.

Total Score: ________
Risk Level: (Circle One):
0 – 3 pts. LOW
4 – 6 pts. MODERATE
7+ pts. HIGHER
Over-Ride? ______ Yes ____ No Over Ride Reason(s): ____ Mental Health _____ Disability _____ Gang Member _____ Flight Risk Other Reason: ______________________________
Final Recommended Risk Level: _______ LOW ________ MODERATE _______ HIGHER

****

FOLLOW-UP DATA Booking Date: ________/_______/__________
Release Date: ________/_______/_____________
Method of Release: _______ Cash Bail ______ Surety Bond _____Court OR Other Release Method: ____

Was Defendant Re-Arrested Prior to Court Disposition? _______ Yes _____No
If Yes, Date of Re-Arrest ________/_______/_________
Most Serious Charge: ____ __________________________
Did Defendant FTA and Have a Warrant Issued? ______ Yes ______ No
If Yes, date of FTA ___________/________/___________
Was Defendant Re-Booked to Jail? _____ Yes _____ No
If Yes, date of Re-Booking: ________/_______/________________
Final Court Dispositions:
Charge Disposition
Date Disposition
Sentence Length

Source: Supreme Court of Nevada Judicial Counsel's Committee to Study Evidence-Based Pretrial Release. (2016). Final report and the Nevada pretrial risk assessment instrument. Retrieved from http://www.ncsl.org/research/civil-and-criminal-justice/pretrial-policy-state-laws-reports-and-resources.aspx.

Information Included in a Pretrial Report

A pretrial report will contain the following information:

- The defendant's demographics and background
- Records from work, school, and/or the military
- National Crime Information Center (NCIC) records and/or jail records
- Driving records
- Sex offender history (if applicable)
- Drug/alcohol use and abuse
- Criminal background information
- The current charge
- Relationships with family, friends, and coworkers
- Financial information
- Medical and mental health records
- A recommendation regarding release
- Recommended release conditions (U.S. Courts, n.d.)

The pretrial officer may include additional information he or she believes to be pertinent to determining if the release of the defendant is appropriate prior to trial. The pretrial report will include a recommendation from the pretrial officer regarding release and will provide an opinion on the likelihood of the defendant committing another crime and returning to court when required (U.S. Courts, n.d.). If the pretrial officer believes the offender is likely to violate another law or to abscond, the officer may recommend the defendant be detained until trial. A sample of questions pretrial officers ask defendants to prepare the pretrial report can be found in Figure 3.2.

Figure 3.2 Pretrial Report Sample Defendant Interview Questions

Demographics

1. What is your full name?
2. Are you married, single, separated, divorced, or widowed? *Note:* If the defendant is male or female and single, skip to 4; otherwise, continue to 3.
3. What is your maiden name?

(Continued)

Figure 3.2 (Continued)

4. Is English your primary language? *Note:* If the defendant's primary language is other than English, continue to 5; otherwise, skip to 7.
5. Are you English literate? *Note:* If the defendant is not English literate, continue to 6; otherwise, skip to 7.
6. Do you want an interpreter?
7. What is your social security number?
8. What is your date of birth?
9. What is your race/ethnicity?
10. Do you have any dependents? *Note:* If the defendant has dependents, continue to 11; otherwise, skip to 12.
11. How many of your dependents live with you?
12. Where were you born? *Note:* If the defendant was not born in the U.S., continue to 13; otherwise, the demographics section is complete.
13. Are you a U.S. citizen? *Note:* If the defendant is not a U.S. citizen, continue to 14; otherwise, the demographics section is complete.
14. Do you have legal documentation such as a Visa, Resident Alien Card (green card), or Employment Authorization Document (work permit)?

Aliases

1. Do you go by any other name?
2. Have you ever been arrested under any other name?

Residence

1. What is your current address?
2. What is your residence status—do you own, rent, pay room and board, live in a hotel/motel, live with family/friend, or another status?
3. How long have you lived there?
4. Is this also your mailing address? *Note:* If mailing address is different, continue to 5; otherwise, skip to 6.
5. What is your mailing address?
6. How long have you lived in the area?
7. How long have you lived in the state?
8. What is your phone number and what type of phone is it: cellular, home, pager, work, friend/relative, or other?

9. Who do you live with? *Note:* If the defendant lives with someone, continue to 10; otherwise, skip to 11.
10. What is that person's relationship to you?
11. Will you be allowed to return to this address when released? If no, where do you plan to live? *Note:* If current address is less than 1 year, continue to 12; otherwise, the residence section is complete.
12. What was your previous address?
13. How long did you live there?

Family/Reference

1. Who can you list as a reference to verify this information?
2. What is that person's relationship to you?
3. What is his/her phone number?
4. What phone number can he/she be reached at today?
5. Where does he/she live?

Employment

1. Were you employed at the time of your arrest? *Note:* If defendant was employed, continue to 2; otherwise, skip to 11.
2. Who do you work for?
3. What is the company's address?
4. What is your supervisor's name and phone number?
5. When did you start working there?
6. When was the last time you worked?
7. What type of work do you do?
8. Does the company know of your arrest and where you are?
9. If necessary, do we have your permission to contact your employer?
10. What is your net monthly income (take home pay)?
11. Within the past 2 years, how many periods of unemployment have you had? *Note:* If defendant was employed at the time of the arrest, the employment section is complete.
12. When was the last time you worked?
13. Who did you work for?
14. How long did you work there?
15. Were you the primary caregiver for a child (stay at home parent) at the time of your arrest?

(*Continued*)

Figure 3.2 (Continued)

Education

1. Are you able to read English?
2. Are you able to write English?
3. Are you currently a student? *Note:* If the defendant is currently a student, continue to 4; otherwise, skip to 6.
4. Are you a full-time or part-time student?
5. How long have you been a student?
6. What is the last grade you completed?
7. What is the name of the current or last school you attended?

Military

1. Have you ever served in the military? *Note:* If the defendant has served in the military, continue to 2; otherwise, the military section is complete.
2. What branch did you serve in?
3. What type of discharge did you receive?
4. When did you serve?
5. Are you eligible for VA benefits?

Substance Use

1. What drugs have you ever used? *Note:* If the defendant reports to drug use immediately or after follow-up questioning, continue to 2; otherwise, skip to 9. Note the responses to 2–8 for each drug reported.
2. When was the last time you used this drug?
3. How often do you use it (or how often did you use it if not currently using)?
4. How long have you been using it (or how long did you use it if not currently using)?
5. How old were you the first time you used this drug?
6. How many times have you used this drug in the last 30 days?
7. Is this your primary drug of choice?
8. Are you interested in substance abuse treatment?
9. Have you ever consumed alcohol? *Note:* If the defendant reports to alcohol consumption immediately or after follow-up questioning, continue to 10; otherwise, the substance use section is complete.
10. When was the last time you consumed alcohol?
11. How often do you drink (or how often did you drink if not currently consuming)?
12. How long have you been drinking alcohol (or how long did you drink alcohol if not currently consuming)?

13. How old were you the first time you consumed alcohol?
14. How many times have you consumed alcohol in the last 30 days? *Note:* If it appears that the defendant may have an alcohol abuse problem, continue to 15; otherwise, the substance use section is complete.
15. Is this your primary drug of choice?
16. Are you interested in alcohol abuse treatment?

Substance Treatment

1. Have you ever participated in any alcohol- or other drug-related treatment? *Note:* If the defendant reports to participating in treatment, continue to 2; otherwise, the substance treatment section is complete. For each occurrence of treatment, complete 2–8 below.
2. What type of treatment was it (detoxification, outpatient, residential, etc.)?
3. What was the primary drug you received treatment for?
4. What was the secondary drug you received treatment for?
5. Did you complete the treatment?
6. Where did you attend treatment?
7. When did you attend treatment?
8. How did you enter the program (court ordered, employment directed, voluntary, or other)?

Health Issues

1. Do you have a physical or mental health issue? *Note:* If the defendant reports a physical or mental health issue, continue to 2; otherwise, the health issues section is complete. Document the responses to 2 and 3 for each reported health issue.
2. Are you currently under a doctor's care? If yes, who/where?
3. What medications do you take to treat this issue?

Criminal Events

1. Do you have any charges pending against you in any criminal or traffic court other than those related to this arrest?
2. Do you have any outstanding warrants (are you wanted anywhere)?
3. What crimes have you been convicted of as an adult? *Note:* If the defendant reports being convicted of a crime as an adult, continue to 4; otherwise, skip to 7. Complete 4 and 5 for each conviction reported.
4. Where were you convicted?
5. When were you convicted?
6. Have you ever been convicted of failure to appear?
7. Are you currently under community supervision (pretrial, local or state probation, ASAP, etc.)?

Source: Virginia Department of Criminal Justice Services. (n.d.). Pretrial services. Retrieved from https://www.dcjs.virginia.gov/sites/dcjs.virginia.gov/files/publications/corrections/virginia-pretrial-investigation-guide.pdf.

Finally, the pretrial report will provide conditions for release. The conditions are tailored to each defendant and typically include the least restrictive rules that allow the offender to remain in the community while not being a threat to the community. Example conditions may include maintaining employment, attending drug or alcohol counseling, going to school, not associating with known felons, drug testing, and so forth (U.S. Courts, n.d.). The pretrial officer can also recommend electronic monitoring and restrictions on travel. Table 3.2 provides information from the National Institute of Justice on the material provided by a pretrial officer and where the officer may get the information reported to the court.

Table 3.2 Information Used to Inform the Court on Release Decisions

- By providing reliable information to the courts, pretrial services programs can enhance the ability of judicial officers to make fair, equitable, and effective pretrial release/detention decisions.
- Pretrial services programs should collect and provide to the court at least the following information about newly arrested defendants:
    - Identity, including date of birth and gender
    - Community ties, including residence, employment, and family status
    - Physical and mental condition, including information concerning abuse of alcohol or drugs
    - Criminal record, including history of adjudications of delinquency
    - Prior record of compliance with conditions of release, including record of appearing for scheduled court dates
- Cases involving charges of domestic violence pose particular challenges for courts and for pretrial services programs. Pretrial services programs can help judicial officers make release/detention decisions in these cases by obtaining and presenting the following information:
    - The defendant's relationship with the alleged victim, including living situation and whether they have children in common
    - The possible existence of any court orders (past or current) restraining the defendant from contacting the victim
    - Substance abuse problems of the defendant
    - Possible living arrangements separate from the alleged victim that may be available for the defendant if released
    - Mechanisms that can be used to prevent contact between the defendant and the alleged victim during the pretrial period and to monitor the defendant's conditions of release
- In addition to information about defendants, pretrial services programs should also obtain and provide to the court information about available supervisory options.

- Defendants are primary sources of information about themselves. They should be interviewed very shortly after arrest to begin the process of gathering and verifying essential information prior to the defendant's first court appearance.
- When interviewing defendants, pretrial services program staff should advise them about the purposes of the interview, the neutral role of the pretrial services agency, the types of information to be collected, how the information will be used, and the fact that their participation in the interview is voluntary.
- Other sources—including the pretrial services program's own records of prior cases involving the same defendant, other criminal justice agencies, motor vehicle departments, the defendant's family members, and the defendant's employer—can provide information about the defendant and can verify information provided in interviews with defendants. If information cannot be verified, it should be clearly labeled as unverified in the program's report to the court.
- The pretrial services program should analyze the information it collects to assess the risks of nonappearance and dangerousness. The risk assessment provides a basis for formulating recommendations concerning conditions of release and the use of available supervisory mechanisms.

Source: U.S. Department of Justice. (2001). Pretrial services programs: Responsibilities and potential. National Institute of Justice, Issues and Practices. Retrieved from https://www.ncjrs.gov/pdffiles1/nij/181939.pdf.

Writing the Pretrial Report

The pretrial report is written in third person and completed, most often, after the pretrial officer interviews the defendant and accumulates the necessary records to verify the information provided by the defendant. The pretrial officer has limited time to write the pretrial report (typically 48–72 hours from the time the accused person was detained), so he or she has to work rather quickly. The format of the pretrial report usually includes double spacing with headings identifying each of the categories of information. Agencies typically provide a template that can be used by pretrial officers, which allows officers to follow the same format for each case, while only modifying the specific facts pertinent to a single case. Once written, the pretrial report is provided to the appropriate judicial officer.

The judicial officer, usually a judge or magistrate, will make a final decision to release or detain the defendant upon receipt of the pretrial report. If released, it is likely the defendant will have several conditions to follow prior to a court trial. If detained, the defendant will remain in jail until his or her court date. Prior to the trial, the charges may be dropped, and pretrial supervision and services will end. However, if the defendant proceeds to court for trial, the case will be decided at trial, and the defendant will be adjudicated or not adjudicated. If adjudicated, a probation officer will become involved in the case prior to sentencing. The probation officer's role will include writing a presentence investigation report.

Reports written by pretrial officers can also be used by other agencies in criminal justice. Jails can use the reports for inmate classification and for drug or alcohol detoxification services. Probation departments may use the reports to avoid duplicating the activities necessary to get information for the presentence investigation report and to determine how successful the individual was on pretrial release. Police departments can use the reports to serve warrants on defendants that do not appear for court and to monitor medium- and high-risk offenders on pretrial release. Researchers can use the reports to identify trends in pretrial release, characteristics of offenders who are likely to be successful or unsuccessful on pretrial release, and to advise on policy and decision making (U.S. Department of Justice, 2001).

Presentence Investigation Reports

Probation officers become involved in cases after adjudication or a guilty finding. Like pretrial service officers, probation officers are tasked with protecting the community and investigating convicted persons. Additionally, probation officers supervise individuals convicted of crimes (U.S. Courts, n.d.), although probation officers may also supervise individuals released from prison in jurisdictions that do not utilize parole. One of their many responsibilities is to prepare a presentence investigation report that provides information to the court on appropriate sentencing.

The presentence investigation report is written immediately following a guilty verdict from a criminal trial and prior to the sentencing hearing. The report is very similar to the pretrial report in that it provides information on the offender's demographics and background; family and friend relationships; previous drug or alcohol use, abuse, and treatment; the current offense; prior convictions; and home, school, and work environments. The presentence investigation report may also rely on a risk/needs assessment using the LSI-R or another assessment tool, and will most likely provide information on the eight criminogenic risk factors associated with the likelihood of reoffending. These risk factors are an offender's history of antisocial behavior, antisocial personality patterns, antisocial cognition, antisocial associates, family and/or marital status, school and/or work status, leisure and/or recreation activities, and substance abuse (Andrew, Bonta, & Wormith, 2006). It is believed that if we target these risk factors, the court will have the greatest success in preventing recidivism. Review Figure 3.3 to understand how the criminogenic risk factors are incorporated into a presentence investigation report.

The presentence investigation report also provides information on sentencing guidelines, the crime's impact on the victim, and the ability of the offender to pay fines and court costs, and allows the probation officer to recommend release conditions that are tailored to the offender's rehabilitative needs (U.S. Courts, n.d.).

Basic reporting skills such as the who, what, when, where, and how are used to write the presentence investigation report (Administrative Office of the U.S. Courts, 1984). The report usually follows a template provided by the probation office or determined by legislation. It is single spaced with headings identifying each of the areas discussed. Statements made in the presentence investigation report are supported with documentation and records, as well as a risk and needs assessment.

The presentence investigation report includes information obtained from interviewing the offender, using questions like those provided in Figure 3.2, and the victim as well as family, friends, and coworkers of the offender.

The probation officer will also request school and work records, mental health and treatment records, and prior criminal, driving, and credit histories, and will review sentencing guidelines on the crime, if any exist, to verify the information provided by the interviewees and the facts of the case. The probation officer will consider treatment and rehabilitative programs in the geographical area that are applicable to the offender's needs and recommend these as conditions for probation in the presentence investigation report.

Information Included in the Presentence Investigation Report

Although many probation offices and state legislatures have requirements on the information included in the presentence investigation report, the report is tailored to each individual offender. According to the Administrative Office of the U.S. Courts (1984, p. 6), the presentence investigation report typically follows the format provided below:

1. **Offense (Core)**

Prosecution version

Victim impact statement

Defendant's version

Codefendant information

Statement of witnesses and complainants

2. **Prior Record (Core)**

Juvenile adjudications

Adult record

3. **Personal and Family Data (Core)**

Defendant

Parents and siblings

Marital

Education

Employment

Health

Physical

Mental and emotional

Military service

Financial condition

Assets

Liabilities

4. **Evaluation (Core)**

Probation officer's assessment

Parole guideline data

Sentencing data
Special sentencing provisions

5. **Recommendation (Core)**
Recommendation and rationale
Voluntary surrender

If a section in the required format does not apply, the probation officer will either delete the subheading and/or write "not applicable." If the offender is convicted of a sex offense or has previous sex offense convictions, the probation officer will include additional information on the sexual victimization of the offender, if any; the sexual treatment history; and information from any other agencies that have worked with the offender in the past. Figure 3.3 provides a common format for presentence investigation reports with explanations of how the probation officer gets the information for the various sections of the report.

Figure 3.3 Common Format for Presentence Investigation Reports

Introductory Headings

To: Honorable Judge of the Court (name)

Defendant: (name)

From: Probation Officer (name) and Office

Address

DOB:

State's Atty: (name) Address:

Defendant's residence: (If incarcerated, indicates where, and lists most recent community address.)

Defense Atty: (name)

Offense: Convicted Offense(s)

Date:

Docket #:

Adjudication:

Include the following headings in the PSI Report:

Plea Agreement: Copy from the signed Plea Agreement

Complaint: Copy the State's Attorney Information, including statutory penalty

Offense Summary:

This is a concise and factual summary of the affidavit. In many cases, it may be important to contact the State's Attorney to determine whether the affidavit has been redacted at the time of the change of plea. Do not attach a copy of the affidavit or retype the affidavit in place of summarizing the offense.

Defendant's Statement:

Ask the defendant for their version of the offense and the circumstances that led up to the offense. It is important to include all factors, including the attitude of the defendant, premeditation of the offense, statements of remorse/acceptance of responsibility or expressions of denial, including acknowledgment or denial of specific allegations, and minimization of harm to the victim and community.

Victim Impact Statement:

Work with local Victim Advocates in contacting victims and requesting statements or interviews. Refer to the victim either by full name or by initials in the victim impact statement, depending on how the victim is referred to in the affidavit. Minors will always be referred to by initials only. Include the victim's report of financial, emotional, and physical consequences resulting from the offense. If the victim is a child, a statement by their parent or guardian may be used in lieu of the victim's statement.

Prior Conviction/Substantiated Abuse Record:

Request and include a current [state] conviction record. Include a record check from other states if the defendant has spent time out of [state]. List the state, name of convicted offense, the date and disposition. In cases involving violence or sexual deviance, review and summarize any [state] Department for Children & Families (DCF) or Department of Disabilities, Aging & Independent Living (DAIL) records to determine if there are prior substantiations of abuse of children or abuse or exploitation of vulnerable adults. Question the defendant regarding the specifics of prior convictions. Review with the defendant behavior patterns that potentially increase risk; e.g., offense type, progression of seriousness, frequency, alcohol/drug involvement, etc.

Prior Supervision/Incarceration History:

Indicate if there is no history with DOC. Summarize any prior community supervision, including any violations of probation or parole, and disciplinary reports while incarcerated. Summarize treatment the defendant may have engaged in while incarcerated or under previous probation or parole supervision. Summarize any graduated sanctions received. Note how cases were discharged (satisfactorily or unsatisfactorily). Contact previous supervising officer(s) in and out of state. If you have information about any juvenile supervision history, add that here.

Social History:

This is a concise factual narrative of the defendant's history, with a discussion of those areas which are relevant to sentencing or casework issues.

Family History:

Provide a concise description of the defendant's family of origin and/or with whom the defendant grew up. Describe the defendant's current relationship with their parents and siblings

(Continued)

Figure 3.3 (Continued)

and indicate if the defendant perceives the relationship as supportive or non-supportive. Include information about the number and nature of dependents, especially young children, or special needs of individuals living in the household.

Education:

Provide the defendant's level of education, their behavior while in school, and any special accommodations (e.g., IEP.)

Marital or Equivalent:

Indicate marital or long-term relationship status, including the defendant's satisfaction with this relationship. State how long the defendant has lived with their current partner, and list previous significant relationships, if applicable. For crimes of domestic violence, include any history of relief from abuse orders, including details of their grounds, and any history of Violation of Abuse Prevention Orders (VAPOs).

Residence:

Provide a concise description of the defendant's current housing situation, including location, whether they rent or own, and if they have roommates or not. Describe the defendant's residential stability, indicating how long they have been at the current address and how long at previous addresses. Describe the defendant's relationship to the people with whom they live.

Employment:

Describe the defendant's current employment circumstances and how long employed at their present job, including their annual earnings. It may be important to ask for pay stubs and/or talk with the defendant's employer. Describe significant employment history, including what types of jobs the defendant has held and the duration of the jobs. If necessary, fill out the Request for Social Security Earnings Information and send to the address on the form. However, do not hold up your submission of the PSI waiting for the return of information. Describe any employment training or professional degrees or licenses. List places, dates, and reason for termination. Note any comments supervisors have made regarding the defendant's reliability and work performance. Note periods of unemployment. Note whether the defendant's employment creates a risk to others.

Financial:

Describe the defendant's assets and liabilities, including property and credit card debt and whether the defendant is self-supporting and contributes to the support of their family. Describe the defendant's ability to make restitution to the victim, or pay for any required treatment and supervision fees.

Military:

Indicate if the defendant served in the military or other national service, and list dates of service, discharge status, and job duties. If necessary, fill out the Request for Military Records form and include it with the PSI. However, do not hold up your submission of the PSI waiting for the return of information.

Medical/Health Status:

Briefly describe any major medical issues, including mental health and developmental disabilities, that the defendant has that may impact on supervision, incarceration, or treatment. Indicate if the defendant is in good health. Note if the defendant is on any medications and what type. Briefly describe any relevant treatment or counseling the defendant is undergoing for health or psychological issues.

Alcohol/Drug History:

List current drug or alcohol use. Describe any prior alcohol and drug use by the defendant, including when they first used alcohol or drugs and what substances. Indicate any problem(s) alcohol and/or drugs have caused in the defendant's life. If the defendant uses drugs, indicate their drug of choice. If the defendant abuses substances, indicate the time of their last use. Indicate any previous treatment efforts for substance abuse. Has the defendant been to residential treatment or participated in AA or NA, and, if so, for how long? What is the defendant's own assessment of the effectiveness of treatment efforts? If there is no problem with substance abuse, state in this section that there is no problem.

Collateral Interviews:

This is the place for any information gained from interviewing family, friends, employers, and others in the defendant's life that is not already included under other sections above.

Results of Assessments:

Provide a narrative explanation of the numerical results of assessment tools (e.g., LSI-R), including an examination of key risk areas, and a summary of any Court-ordered clinical assessments. Establish if the defendant will be classified Level A or Level B for purposes of correctional programming, if incarcerated. Note: Offender responses to LSI questions 53 & 54 about their sentence should not be referenced in the narrative.

Summary:

Briefly summarize the major points of the report, but do not present new information in this section. Include both positive and negative factors in the defendant's life. Present your conclusions in a logical fashion based upon your research and data.

Program/Condition Options for Judge:

Address whether the seriousness of the crime precludes a probationary sentence, and whether the defendant's risk of re-offense can be managed in the community. The sentencing recommendation must address what will be required while the person is incarcerated or under community supervision. Consider restorative justice processes, especially in cases in which the Department is recommending probation, including referral to a community reparative board or justice center as a condition of probation.

- If the defendant is likely to be incarcerated or ordered into residential treatment, and is in a custodial role for one or more dependents, include a statement about how care will be provided for the dependents. Adverse effects on the family are not reason to recommend against residential treatment or incarceration, but require planning to deal with the situation.

(Continued)

Figure 3.3 (Continued)

- A recommendation, which includes community supervision, must address conditions of probation needed to manage risk, protect the victim, and mandate any required treatment. A recommendation, which includes incarceration, must identify any specific DOC program and the minimum length of sentence required to be eligible for that program.

NOTE: ONLY IF REQUESTED BY THE COURT, the PSI Investigator will include a recommended minimum and maximum term of incarceration or a minimum and maximum term of suspended sentence.

Source: State of Vermont Agency of Human Services Department of Corrections. (2011). Pre-sentence investigation reports. Retrieved from http://doc.vermont.gov/about/policies/rpd/correctional-services-301-550/335-350-district-offices-general/copy_of_342-01-pre-sentence-investigation-psi-reports.

Most jurisdictions require a risk and needs assessment to be attached to the presentence investigation report. This evaluation is separate from the pretrial assessment but may include many of the same measurements. As with the pretrial risk and needs assessment, the presumption is that the higher the score, the more likely the offender will be a risk to the community and will likely reoffend.

Once completed, the presentence investigation report is provided to the offender and his or her counsel prior to the sentencing hearing and in enough time for them to review it and request corrections. The offender and his or her counsel can provide testimony at the sentencing hearing to refute or minimize information in the report. The judge will rule on whether to accept the change, deny the change based on provided facts, or not consider the refuted information during sentencing (Administrative Office of the U.S. Courts, 1984). The probation officer who wrote the report will likely testify to the information as well at the sentencing hearing. Finally, the judge uses the information in the report to determine the appropriate sentence for the offender.

Exercise 3.1

Using Figure 3.3, write a presentence investigation report by interviewing a friend. Pretend you are the probation officer and your friend is an offender convicted of a felony assault.

If the offender receives a sentence of incarceration, the presentence investigation report is sent to the state or federal correctional system to be placed in the offender's file. The report is used to assist in inmate classification, as well as treatment and rehabilitation while incarcerated. Later, the presentence investigation report can be used by the parole board to determine parole release and conditions. If parole exists in the state where the offender is incarcerated, the parole officer will also use the report to make recommendations on the conditions of parole and while monitoring the offender. If the offender receives a sentence of probation, the report is used as a guide for the probation officer to monitor the offender while on probation.

Contact Sheets and Revocation Petitions

Some states and the federal government do not have a formal parole system. At the federal level and in these states, probation officers monitor both offenders prior to incarceration and offenders after incarceration. If an offender is allowed supervised release, the probation or parole officer monitoring the offender will create other reports about the offender. In many cases, the case reports already developed about the offender can be shared from one agency to another or one officer to another, and between criminal justice agencies and non-criminal justice agencies through case management software (CMS). When agencies are integrated with one another, they can ensure the information being shared is secure and remains updated as the case moves through case processing (Brown, n.d.).

A report often used during case processing is a contact sheet. A contact sheet is simply a record of meetings and discussions with the offender and others who report information to the officer about the offender. Contact sheets are offender specific. Contact sheets can be kept electronically but are often handwritten, single spaced, and attached to the inside cover of the offender's file.

Information Included on the Contact Sheet

On the contact sheet, the officer will typically include the date of the contact and a general summary of what was discussed, what happened, and/or what was recommended. For example, if a probation officer had a monthly meeting with the offender and discussed family issues as well as a shoplifting diversion program, the officer would record the date and time of the meeting and a summary of both the family issues brought forth by the offender and the shoplifting diversion program information along with any comments made by the offender. The resulting notes may look like Figure 3.4.

Although not written by the probation or parole officer, the offender's file may also include other self-report documents from the offender and from counselors or other individuals working at agencies where the offender may be attending programs. The file may contain urinalysis reports if the offender is required to submit to drug testing. These documents are used by the probation or parole officer to determine if the offender is meeting the conditions of release.

Information Included in a Revocation Petition

If, over time, it is determined that the offender is not following the stipulations ordered by the court, a probation or parole officer can request a revocation of supervised release. In this instance, an officer will file a revocation petition that informs the court that the offender is violating the conditions ordered. The revocation petition is available as a fill-in-the-blank template to probation and parole officers. The officer will complete the appropriate blanks by providing the requested information in full and complete sentences. An example revocation petition is found in Figure 3.5.

Upon review of the petition, the court can take no action, summon the defendant to court, and/or revoke the probation or parole. The court can also modify the conditions of probation or parole if they do not exceed the stipulations that could have been ordered at the time of sentencing. An offender could be incarcerated as a result of revocation. In this case, the probation or parole officer would close his or her file on the offender.

Figure 3.4 Contact Sheet Example

Name:______Mark Smith______________________________________Case #:___MC067-2019_______

Date/Time/Location of Contact	Notes
2-28-2019 10:00 a.m. - Henderson County Probation Office	Mark Smith visited the probation office for a 30-minute appointment at 10:00 a.m. on 2-28-2019. Mark discussed issues at home, to include his wife not working, stress with getting the kids to do homework and to attend school, not having the money to pay bills and being overdue on electric and water by two months. Mark stated that he needs a higher paying job and has concerns that he is going under. Mark discussed not having the money to pay for the shoplifting diversion class he is ordered to attend on 3-15-2019. I recommended that he look for another job and recommended several places that hire felons at a higher pay rate than he currently makes. I also recommended potential jobs for his wife and discussed daycare options for after school for the kids. I agreed to make a call to a local tire shop where I've successfully placed felons before for employment. I also agreed to help his wife complete an application if she needs assistance. I will check with shoplifting diversion to see if we can reschedule the class for April 2019.
3-4-2019 1:50 p.m. - phone call	Contact was made with Ada Roe at shoplifting diversion and Mark is scheduled to attend the course beginning 4-21-2019. I called Mark and provided him with the new date and mailed a letter to him with the date and location. I left a message with Tires Plus regarding available positions. Awaiting a call back.

Source: Author created.

Figure 3.5 Example Revocation of Supervised Release Petition

CR-300

SUPERVISING AGENCY *(Name and address):* TELEPHONE NO.: FAX NO. *(Optional):* E-MAIL ADDRESS *(Optional):*	*FOR COURT USE ONLY*
SUPERIOR COURT OF CALIFORNIA, COUNTY OF STREET ADDRESS: CITY AND ZIP CODE: BRANCH NAME:	
IN THE MATTER OF *(name of supervised person):* Date of birth:	
PETITION FOR REVOCATION ☐ **PAROLE (Pen. Code, §§ 3000.08, 1203.2)** ☐ **PRCS (Pen. Code, §§ 3455, 1203.2)** ☐ **PROBATION (Pen. Code, § 1203.2)** ☐ **MANDATORY SUPERVISION (Pen. Code, §§ 1170(h)(5)(B), 1203.2)**	SUPERVISING AGENCY NUMBER: COURT/CASE NUMBER:

INSTRUCTIONS

- *Before filing this form, petitioner should consult local rules and court staff to schedule the hearing in item 1.*
- *Petitioner must note whether the petition applies to a parole (beginning July 1, 2013), postrelease community supervision, probation, or mandatory supervision matter by marking the appropriate check box above.*

1. **HEARING INFORMATION:** A hearing on this petition for revocation has been scheduled as follows:

   Date: Time: Dept.:
   Location *(if different than court address above):*

   If an interpreter is needed, please specify the language:

2. **CUSTODY STATUS *(Select one):*** ☐ not in custody ☐ in custody *(specify location):*
   Booking number *(if any):*

3. **CONVICTION INFORMATION:**
   The supervised person was originally convicted of the following offenses:

   on *(date):* in case numbers *(specify):*
   in county of *(specify):* and sentenced to *(specify sentence):*

4. **SUPERVISION INFORMATION:** The supervised person was released on supervision on *(specify date):*
   Name of current supervising agent or officer:
   Supervision is scheduled to expire on (i.e., the controlling discharge date is) *(date):*

5. **SPECIFIC TERMS AND CONDITIONS:** Petitioner alleges that the supervised person has violated the following terms and conditions of supervision *(if more space is needed, please use* Attachment to Judicial Council Form *(MC-025)):*

6. **SUMMARY:** The supervising agency established probable cause for the alleged violation on *(date):*
   The circumstances of the alleged violation are *(if more space is needed, please use* Attachment to Judicial Council Form *(MC-025)):*

7. **SPECIAL PAROLE STATUS** *(check this box **only if** the supervised person is subject to parole under Penal Code section 3000.1):*
   ☐ The supervised person is on parole under Penal Code section 3000.1. If the court determines that the person has violated parole, the court is required to remand the person to the custody of CDCR for future parole consideration. (Pen. Code, § 3000.08(h).)

I declare under penalty of perjury and to the best of my information and belief that the foregoing is true and correct.

Date: ______________________ By ______________________
NAME AND TITLE OF PETITIONER SIGNATURE OF PETITIONER

Page 1 of 1

Form Approved for Optional Use
Judicial Council of California
CR-300 [Rev. January 1, 2015]

PETITION FOR REVOCATION
(Pen. Code, §§ 1170(h)(5)(B), 1203.2, 3000.08, and 3455)

www.courts.ca.gov

For your protection and privacy, please press the Clear This Form button after you have printed the form.

Print this form | Save this form | Clear this form

Source: Judicial Council of California. (2015). CR-300 petition for revocation. Retrieved from https://www.courts.ca.gov/documents/cr300.pdf.

CHAPTER SUMMARY

Pretrial, probation, and parole officers provide similar services to the community: (1) They make recommendations to the court on detaining or releasing offenders, (2) they provide for the safety of the community, and (3) they monitor offenders who are under court supervision. To accomplish these goals, these officers write reports. The reports are most often written using templates provided by agencies or legislators. However, the guide is modified, when necessary, to provide adequate information about specific offenders to the court.

Pretrial officers write pretrial reports to help the court determine the level of risk an accused person presents to the safety of the community if released prior to a criminal trial. The pretrial report can be used by other agencies as well to determine classification, risks, needs, and conditions of release.

Probation officers supervise offenders in the community prior to incarceration. They write presentence investigation reports to assist the court in determining appropriate sentences for offenders. If an offender is provided probation, a probation officer will monitor the offender to ensure he or she completes release conditions ordered by the court. Probation officers also write contact sheets and file revocation petitions if an offender violates the conditions of probation.

Parole officers, like probation officers, also monitor offenders; however, they supervise offenders released after a period of incarceration. Parole officers maintain contact sheets and file revocation petitions if a parolee violates the conditions of parole.

QUESTIONS FOR CONSIDERATION

1. When writing a presentence investigation report, why is it important to include school, medical, and family relationship information? How does this information assist the judge during sentencing?
2. Considering that some pretrial reports must be written within 48–72 hours after arrest, what are some of the challenges a pretrial officer may face in getting the information needed to write the report and in verifying the facts of the report?
3. Why are contact sheets useful for probation and parole officers? Identify at least two reasons.

CHAPTER 4

Incident Reports and Beyond

The nature of the corrections environment mandates that officers document their actions and other incidents in a narrative format. The report narrative written by a corrections officer is very similar to that written by a police officer. Just as a police officer must write a narrative incident report detailing a criminal event or other activity, a corrections officer must often do the same. A narrative report can be used to officially document most events, including inmate criminal activity, violation of institutional policy, discovered contraband, officer and inmate injuries, and incidents between officers and inmates, as well as those between inmates. Agency documents may also be used to justify inmate discipline, segregation, or use of force by an officer.

This chapter introduces students to the most common reports used in a corrections detention setting and strategies for writing the narrative section in those reports.

Writing Well

The need to write well in the criminal justice fields generally and in corrections specifically has never been more important. Quible and Griffin (2007) observed that employers "consistently ranked oral and written education skills as among the most important, if not the most important, qualifications their employees should possess" (p. 32). Additionally, Kleckner and Marshall (2014) observed that "employers rated basic writing mechanics as second in importance among communication skills . . . yet found that the employers' satisfaction level for this skill . . . was the lowest among all communication skills" (p. 180). Furthermore, the intangible costs of deficient writing include image degradation for both the employee and employer, reduced productivity when supervisors and officers must reread and correct poorly written reports, and incorrect decisions based on poorly written reports (Quible & Griffin, 2007, p. 32). An example of this is provided in In the News 4.1. A well-written report will convict criminals, encourage community support, and reflect positively on the employee and the agency.

In the News 4.1

Broward's Jail Healthcare Provider Charged With Doctoring Patient Records About Death

By DAN CHRISTENSEN FloridaBulldog.org
FORT LAUDERDALE, Fla -

Armor Correctional Health Services, the Miami-based company that provides jail healthcare services for Broward, Palm Beach and 18 other Florida counties, has been criminally charged by the state of Wisconsin with seven counts of intentionally falsifying inmate healthcare records.

The criminal complaint alleges that Armor, through its employees, doctored patient records concerning four inmates, including one who died of dehydration while in custody in the Milwaukee County Jail.

The charge accuses Armor Correctional employees of engaging in "a pattern and practice of intentionally falsifying entries in inmate patient health care records."

Three Milwaukee County jail officials were charged with various felonies in connection with an inmate's death. The investigation concluded medical staff might have identified the inmate's fatal medical distress if the medical records were not falsified.

Basic Writing Skills

Like any skill, writing well requires practice and resources. First, one should obtain a useful, current writing style manual, like the one published by the American Psychological Association. Style manuals are easily found in local bookstores and online. One should look for one that is fairly easy to use and purchase the most recent edition available. An excellent online writing resource is the Purdue Online Writing Lab, https://owl.purdue.edu/owl/research_and_citation/apa_style/apa_formatting_and_style_guide/general_format.html. With some research, other online versions can also be found.

Computer spelling programs can be helpful when typing documents, but avoid becoming overly reliant and complacent since these programs will fail to indicate all errors. These programs will not detect improperly used homonyms, for example, such as *there* and *their*, *here* and *hear*, or *too* and *two*.

An English grammar text refreshes writers on matters of punctuation and sentence structure. This text could serve that purpose. Others are more detailed and better suited for academic needs. A writer can use the grammar text in place of friends and family who may volunteer to help with writing and proofreading. Unfortunately, these people may be unavailable when needed or uninformed about proper writing practices. Only the writer bears the responsibility for his or her writing. Remember, it is the writer's signature that appears at the bottom of the document, and responsibility for errors cannot be shifted to someone who provided assistance. Writing tools should be kept within easy reach while writing, proofreading, and editing documents. Writers should use these resources frequently.

Writing for an Audience

Perhaps the most important concept in writing for the criminal justice professions is to always remember who will read the document—the audience. Of course, a supervisor and peers read the reports. Supervisors evaluate an officer's work, investigators use the reports as the foundation for an investigation, and the courts use reports to assess a defendant before and after trial. But a criminal justice document's audience does not stop there. As a public servant, a criminal justice professional's true audience is the citizens served.

Many criminal justice documents become public record, and as such, they are available for all to review. Attorneys, paralegals, and staff personnel on both sides of a case, as well as judges, may also read corrections reports. Imagine if an officer writes a report later read by Justices of the Supreme Court, as they did in 1983. In *Hudson v. Palmer* (1984), Justices read Corrections Officer Hudson's report about the shakedown search of an inmate's cell. Palmer, an inmate at the Bland Correctional Center in Bland, Virginia, alleged that Hudson had violated his right to privacy, illegally searched his cell in violation of the Fourth Amendment, and illegally destroyed his personal property without due process (*Hudson v. Palmer*, 1984). In a landmark ruling supporting corrections, the Court ruled that prisoners have no expectation of privacy in a jail facility or cell, that the search did not violate the Fourth Amendment protection against unreasonable searches, and that destruction of the inmate's property did not violate due process protections since it served a legitimate, institutional interest (*Hudson v. Palmer*, 1984).

Every piece of writing should reflect the writer's best writing effort. Written documents throughout the corrections professions are often the first indicator of professionalism, and sloppy reports give bad images.

Writing Styles

The four academic writing styles are expository, narrative, descriptive, and persuasive. Briefly, the expository style explains a process, the narrative tells a story, the descriptive paints a picture for the audience, and the persuasive tries to convince the audience to agree with the writer's position on a topic. Although corrections reports are not academic writing assignments, nor should they be written or evaluated as such, officers use these writing styles in the narrative section of the incident report. Most often, the narrative of the corrections incident report requires a combination of narrative and descriptive writing styles. These styles are described in this section.

Narration

The dominant writing style in a corrections report narrative is narration. Narratives tell a story by presenting events in an orderly structure and logical sequence (Kirszner & Mandell, 2010) that helps the reader understand the writer's purpose. Events are presented in chronological order beginning with the officer's initial involvement in an incident and ending when the officer concludes his or her role in the case so that readers will understand the sequence of events from beginning to end.

Descriptive

Descriptive is also appropriate for corrections reports since they are required to be detailed and specific about names, times, dates, events, and geographic locations. Descriptive writing uses the five senses—sight, hearing, taste, touch, and smell—to tell the audience the physical nature of a person, place, or thing. In order for the narrative to be convincing, it must include specific details to help create a picture for the reader (Kirszner & Mandell, 2010). In this sense, correctional reports parallel police incident reports. Corrections officers, like police officers, must describe with great detail and accuracy an incident or crime scene, observations of all types, and the result of criminal and often violent behavior.

Eliminate Spelling Errors

Proper spelling is a vital part of every corrections report. Just as improper grammar and punctuation are signs of semi-literacy, so too is improper spelling. A misspelled word screams for the reader's attention and shapes a negative image of the officer, supervisor, and institution. Several misspelled words can have such a negative effect upon the reader that many will simply refuse to continue reading, finding it too difficult to understand the narrative.

Go beyond the spell check. Those who write by hand should keep a good dictionary nearby. Those who write with a computer should never rely solely upon a spell check program to accurately make corrections. While a spell check will identify and correct misspelled words, it will fail to correct homophones. In this phrase, *four example*, the word *four* is misspelled, yet a spell check program would fail to identify the error.

Eliminate Slang and Jargon

Like any other professional, corrections officers develop a way of talking to other officers. The slang, jargon, and even 10 codes of the corrections profession have a way of creeping into reports and speech. This can lead to misinterpretation, though, for those who have no knowledge about the profession. At times, speaking in codes is an advantage, but report writing requires a communication style that conveys information to the reader clearly and concisely.

Table 4.1 lists some of the words most frequently used as corrections jargon. One can usually replace these words with simpler words that people without corrections experience easily understand. If an officer must use a slang or street term, immediately after using the term in the report he or she should include an explanation for the reader. For example, an officer may write about an item of contraband discovered during the search of a

Slang or Jargon	Reader Friendly	Slang or Jargon	Reader Friendly
stated verbalized related	said	altercation physical disturbance mutual combat struggle	fight
transpired	happened	closed fist open fist	fist
exited	got out/left	struck battered contacted	hit
responded to the area of	went to (specific location)	was in possession of possessed	had
initiated/instigated commenced	started	verbal altercation verbal dispute verbal confrontation	argument
attempted made an effort	tried	located/discovered	found
monitored surveilled	watched	observed viewed perceived	saw

Table 4.1 Examples of Common Slang and Jargon Used in Incident Reports

prisoner's cell like this: "I found a shank (common jail terminology for a homemade knife) hidden in the inmate's mattress."

Remember, professional does not mean convoluted or fancy. Officers should write reports in general English that most people can easily understand.

Eliminate Emotion

In face-to-face conversation, emotional content is communicated through tone of voice, facial expression, and body language (Melé, 2009). In written documents, the writer expresses emotion through tone. According to Charles Baldick (1996) in the *Oxford Dictionary of Literary Terms*, tone refers to the author's attitude toward the reader or subject matter. The tone of a narrative "affects the reader just as one's tone of voice affects the listener in everyday exchanges" (Ober, 1995). Writers of criminal justice narratives should strive for an overall tone that reflects an impartial, courteous, fair observer, that contains nondiscriminatory language and an appropriate level of difficulty for the audience (Ober, 1995).

Use a Professional Voice

Professional is a word with which many officers struggle. In the context of the written correctional report, a professional voice refers to the writer's tone and vocabulary. Officers should avoid writing like they talk, instead adopting a more professional voice appropriate for a business report. Professional writing is more structured than speech, uses longer sentences, and is more detailed than conversational speech, which relies on short, simple sentences and few details (Biber & Gray, 2010).

The writer's voice, though, should not attempt to impress readers with a large vocabulary or corrections jargon. An officer would do better to write a clear and easily readable report.

Answer the Interrogatives

Interrogatives introduce questions. They are the *who*, *what*, *when*, *where*, *why*, and *how* required in many criminal justice documents. The following is a partial list of basic interrogatives.

Who

1. Who is the victim, witness, suspect, defendant?
2. Who called the officer or reported the crime?
3. Who are the other officers who assisted your investigation?
4. Who are the medical personnel who treated any injuries?
5. Who discovered the event or crime?
6. Who was the first to arrive at the scene?
7. Who transported the injured to the hospital?
8. Who transported the defendant to medical?
9. Who discovered or recovered the evidence?
10. Who submitted the evidence for retention?
11. To whom was the evidence submitted?
12. Who photographed the crime scene?
13. Who signed the search/arrest warrant?
14. Who authorized the use of the technique/procedure?
15. Who were the backup officers?
16. Who comprised the entry team?

What

1. What is the incident?
2. What happened first?
3. What weapons or tools were used to facilitate the crime?
4. What involvement did the victim have in the incident? Was there any victim/perpetrator confrontation?
5. What happened next?
6. What drugs were used?
7. What name brand chemical presumptive test kit was used to test the drugs?
8. What injuries did the victim receive?
9. What treatment did the injured receive?
10. What observations did you make?
11. What action did you take?
12. What weapons did you use?
13. What questions did you ask the inmate?
14. What is the victim's relationship to the inmate?
15. What property was stolen?
16. What was the motive?

When

1. When did the incident occur?
2. When was the incident first discovered?
3. When was the incident first reported to institutional staff?
4. When did the officer arrive at the scene?
5. When was the evidence discovered?
6. When did the injured receive medical treatment?
7. When was the deceased pronounced dead?
8. When was the arrest made?
9. When was the property impounded/released?

10. When was the inmate interviewed?
11. When did the inmate confess?
12. When was the inmate advised of Miranda rights?
13. When was the stolen property recovered?

Where

1. Where did the incident take place?
2. Where was the inmate at the time of the crime or incident?
3. Where was the inmate found?
4. Where was the evidence found?
5. Where was the evidence submitted for retention/analysis?
6. Where were the witnesses in relation to the incident?
7. Where were the injured treated?
8. Where did the officer conduct any follow-up investigation?
9. Where was lighting located near the scene?
10. Where did the officer receive specialized training for the technique/procedure used?
11. From where did the officer respond?
12. Where was the inmate transported?
13. Where was the inmate interviewed?

Why

1. Why did the crime occur? (motive)
2. Why did the inmate wait to report the crime?
3. Why did the inmate react the way he/she did?
4. Why did the officer respond the way he/she did?
5. Why did the inmate confess?
6. Why is the informant motivated to give information?
7. Why were weapons authorized to be used by officers?
8. Why did the criminal attempt succeed/fail?
9. Why were specialized units requested?
10. Why was the officer involved in the incident?
11. Why is the officer writing this report?

12. Why did the inmate resist restraint?
13. Why was the inmate involved in the crime?
14. Why was the officer in the area of the incident?
15. Why did the officer stop the inmate?
16. Why was the officer in fear?
17. Why did the officer detain the inmate?
18. Why did the officer release the inmate?

How

1. How did the incident occur?
2. How did the inmate gain entry/exit?
3. How was the incident discovered?
4. How was the property removed from the scene?
5. How was the incident reported?
6. How long did the incident last?
7. How was the inmate dressed?
8. How were weapons used?
9. How did the inmate defend himself/herself or flee?
10. How did the officer respond to the inmate's requests for help?
11. How did the confrontation begin/end?
12. How was the inmate subdued/restrained?
13. How was the item removed?
14. How did the injury/death occur?
15. How many officers/units assisted in the investigation?
16. How much contraband was seized?
17. How much did the drugs weigh?

Source: Author created.

Note Taking

Proper note-taking skills are vital to the accuracy of initial and follow-up reports. Note taking is the process of gathering and recording facts and information relevant to an incident. Officers gather a variety of information in a quick and efficient manner so they may recall the facts of the case to write the incident report, assist follow-up investigations, and refresh their memory for court testimony.

Corrections officers often use a small, pocket-sized writing pad for gathering initial notes. Some officers use a digital voice recorder to record notes, crime scene observations, and witness and victim statements.

In practice, field notes should be written in a standard format to record valuable information. The standard format helps officers later when called upon to recall information from on-scene notes. In on-scene notes, officers may make entries with symbols that only they understand and use flexible shorthand to quickly record data. This is perfectly acceptable because only the officer is required to interpret this information from the notes later.

Writing the Narrative

Like any other form of writing, the narrative must have a logical structure to help readers follow the line of reasoning and reach the same or similar conclusion held by the writer. The narrative should have a distinct beginning, middle, and end that consist of an introduction, the body, and a conclusion.

Writing a narrative requires more than just jotting down some information: It is a carefully crafted piece of persuasive writing. Of course, the narrative records data and facts relative to an incident. But it is important that the audience understands the facts of the case, the actions taken by officers, and how and why decisions were made. For example, if a corrections officer discovered contraband in an inmate's possession, the officer must thoroughly and accurately record all pertinent details of the event. The narrative of the document not only must contain all of the vital case information, but it must also be logically constructed.

Criminal justice academic and professional narratives should follow a chronological order of events that have a distinct beginning (introduction), middle (body), and end (conclusion).

The Introduction

The introduction in corrections incident reports is the first paragraph of the document. It is the reader's first exposure to the events about which the officer is writing. In a telephone conversation in which the parties have never met, the callers quickly reach conclusions about each other from voice, word choice, and conversational ability. Readers, too, will quickly form an opinion of the writer's competency as a writer, officer, and investigator from the first few sentences of the document. And this assumption goes well beyond the individual—an officer's reports also present the reader with an image of the criminal justice agency as a whole. Therefore, the officer is obligated personally and professionally to present to the audience the best possible impression. An officer creates this favorable impression not by using fancy words, slang, or jargon. The officer accomplishes a positive impression by presenting the reader with all of the necessary information in a clear and logically presented narrative. A writer should never assume the reader has the same knowledge about the case that he or she does. Therefore, a good introduction starts with a general statement about the case, gives any relevant background information, and focuses upon a thesis statement.

The Thesis Statement

A thesis statement is a clear and concise declaration of the main idea. In addition to helping the reader quickly and easily determine the writing purpose, it should also help the writer focus on the writing task. A clearly written thesis statement focuses the reader's attention upon the writer's topics.

Examples:

1. At about 3:15 PM on 06/01/2018, I responded to cell 2015 when I heard an inmate screaming from inside the cell.
2. On 06/01/2018, while assigned to Pod B control, I saw a fight begin between several inmates in the Pod B common area.

Although some information such as names, dates, times, and locations may be contained in other areas of a document, officers must reintroduce that information in the narrative's introductory paragraph. The narrative should contain enough details so that it can stand alone without the support of information contained in other areas of the paperwork. This idea follows a key concept of this book—writing in a reader-friendly format that promotes communication and understanding. By reintroducing details, the writer helps the reader follow the narrative without having to leave the page and scan another section for pertinent information.

The Body

The separate paragraphs of the narrative's body should each focus upon a single idea or theme. For example, an officer might dedicate separate paragraphs to discuss an incident scene, a victim's statement, stolen property, or suspects.

A writer should use a topic sentence to focus the main idea of each paragraph. Like a thesis statement, the topic sentence helps both the reader and writer concentrate on what is to come. It is often the first sentence of the paragraph and presents the main idea of the paragraph ahead.

A good topic sentence is written clearly and concisely, and it identifies the subject or specific issue to be developed. Without some clearly stated direction, a reader is more likely to become confused about the writing. Just as a writer must present the total narrative in a clear and logical order, the writer must also do so within the paragraph. All of the parts of the document must be coherent and fit together so that it makes sense to the reader.

The structure of sentences within the paragraph can follow several models for a logical presentation. A writer can relate the events in chronological or time order as they happened. Or the writer might give special prominence to some event and leave the most important information for last. Relating the events as they occurred in a chronological, time-ordered fashion is often the simplest and easiest way to do this.

The Conclusion

In the introductory paragraph, a writer would have told the reader what he or she intended to write with a thesis statement. Now, in the conclusion paragraph, the writer must remind the audience of what has been written. A writer can effectively do this by restating the thesis. Rather than simply writing the thesis statement again, though, a writer should retell it in a slightly different fashion. For example, a writer could restate the thesis statement from Example 1 above as follows:

> My investigation concludes the screaming I heard was from Inmate Jones, Allen, who was being kicked and punched by Inmate Smith, Michael.

Formatting the Incident Report

The Beginning

Paragraph 1

1. Background information
    a. Date
    b. Time
    c. Officers involved
    d. Assigned location
    e. Office building
    f. Room or office number
    g. Facility name
    h. Type of call

The Middle

Paragraph 2
What happened when you arrived?

1. What did you see?
    a. Use descriptive language to paint an overall picture of the scene.
2. How many subjects? (Use a separate paragraph to describe each subject.)
    a. A brief description of the subjects
        i. Gender
        ii. Race
        iii. Any blood or other evidence of injuries?
3. In a single sentence, what did the first reporter or witness tell you?

Paragraph 3 (If needed, add additional paragraphs for each subject following the format for Paragraph 2.)

Paragraph 4
Describe your sensory perception of the scene.

1. What did you hear?
   a. Arguing, talking
      i. What was the subject saying?
2. What did you see?
   a. Fighting or wrestling
      i. Describe in detail (punching, kicking, biting, throwing objects)
      ii. Drinking alcohol
      iii. Injuries
      iv. Evidence
      v. Other disruptive or illegal behavior
      vi. Describe in detail
3. What did you smell?
   a. Alcohol
   b. Marijuana
   c. Urine or feces
   d. Decomposition
   e. Other odors
4. What did you touch?
   a. Items that were hot or cold
   b. Weather conditions (rain, snow, wind, etc.)
   c. Room temperature

Paragraph 5
What did you do?

1. Approach, detain, separate, interview subjects
2. Interviews
   a. Tell the subject's version of the event.
   b. What did witnesses tell you?
3. What did you do?
4. Call for assistance or supervisor?
5. Collect evidence?
   a. Photographs
   b. Other items of value
6. Paperwork?
   a. Obtain sworn, written statements
   b. Witness statements
   c. Other official forms

Table 4.2 Incident Report Writing Checklist

Writing Process	Organization	Format	General Writing	Grammar
Note taking—gather the facts	Use a distinct beginning, middle, and end	First person	Answer who, what, when, where, why, how	Use standard grammar
Write the first draft	Thesis statement	Active voice	Use names—not labels (victim, witness, suspect)	No spelling errors
Edit for grammar errors	Each paragraph uses a topic sentence	Past tense		No punctuation errors
Edit for writing errors	Each paragraph focuses on a single idea	Chronological order		No abbreviations
Edit for organization errors				No sentence structure errors (fragments, run-ons, comma splices)
Write the final draft				

Source: Author created.

7. Arrest information (if applicable)?
   a. Name of official charge
   b. State statute number
   c. Who transported the subject to medical?
   d. How was the subject transported to medical?

The End

Paragraph 6
What did you do after the incident?

1. Submit evidence?
2. Make any notifications?
3. Any other official action that you took

Editing

There are three parts to the writing process: prewriting or planning, writing, and rewriting or editing. Every written document should be edited. Editing is often more than simply proofreading for basic errors. For many writers, editing involves major structural and thematic revisions.

This type of major writing surgery is very easy for officers who are fortunate enough to write criminal justice documents with a computer. Studies have found computer-aided writers make more changes to their work and revise at all stages of their writing (Carole & Richard, 1988). Rather than waiting to revise until the project is completed, as do most hand writers, the computer-aided writer effectively revises while writing. Menu bar and function key options that aid editing and revision include spell check, grammar check, format, text insert and delete, and text-scanning methods.

While many writers fear the blank page and find getting started difficult, the computer, with all its writer's aids, seems to invite writing since the text is manipulated on the screen before it even touches the page. And once the writer understands the function keys, moving through the text to revise becomes easier. Rather than writing and erasing, or sometimes starting all over as in a handwritten document, the insert, delete, and move text functions can make revision easier.

Those who write by hand can still effectively edit their work and submit well-written, organized, and error-free reports. Editing should be done at three levels to include word-level, sentence-level, and global revisions.

Word-Level Editing

A writer should never go to work without a bag of writing tools. Basic writing tools should include a dictionary (either a paperback version or an electronic model), a thesaurus, and this book or another grammar or writing handbook.

Even though a thesaurus is useful, a writer should be cautious when using one. A writer should not overly rely on the thesaurus as a tool to eliminate repetition of key words or phrases in reports. While a thesaurus is a useful tool, it can, like anything else, be abused. An experienced reader will quickly spot dependence and view this as a weakness in word choice and writing skills.

Sentence-Level Editing

A writer should scan the document narrative quickly but thoroughly, paying particular attention to sentence structure problems such as run-ons, comma splices, and fragments. He or she should also consult a grammar book for questions concerning sentence structure, the use of commas, and other structural devices that may not be familiar. Effective writers often seek resources such as these to help correct and improve their writing.

Global Editing

Rereading the narrative again, paying particular attention to structure and organization, is imperative. The writer should ask if it has a clear beginning, middle, and end to the incident report. Is there a clear thesis statement in the introduction and a restatement of the thesis in the conclusion? Is the body logically structured with each paragraph focusing on a single main topic? Is each paragraph focused and introduced by using a clearly written topic sentence? If not, the writer should make any necessary changes.

A writer should never write anything without first planning the structure of the work. The type of incident being documented will often dictate the structure of the report. Sometimes a writer will be able to decide what format to follow while, other times, he or she may not. The only rule to follow here is that the organization is logical and easy for readers to follow.

When editing for content, a writer should read the report first from beginning to end while asking himself or herself the six interrogative questions: *who*, *what*, *when*, *where*, *why*, and *how*. The writer should read quickly but efficiently to determine if he or she has answered everything that someone unfamiliar with the event would want to know. Is there anything more that could be added that would make the document more complete and easier to understand? Any omissions should be corrected at this point.

Types of Reports

Incident Reports

The incident report is a common writing assignment in corrections professions. The purpose of the narrative is to convey information to the audience in a clear, concise, and grammatically correct manner. In the narrative section of this report, the officer becomes a storyteller and has the opportunity to relate the details of the event, observations, and actions. The narrative is the most crucial and important part of any criminal justice document.

Incident Report Examples

The following are offered as general examples of how a well-written corrections incident report might be written. Officers must, of course, follow

Table 4.3 Content Checklist (Be sure to include this information in the incident report.)

Incident	Inmate	Staff Member	Infraction
Date and time	Name	Charging member name	Infraction code
Location	Identity number	Charging member job code	Infraction type
	Enemy level	Witness names	Infraction severity
	Inmate statement		Infraction narrative
	Inmate plea		
	Inmate demeanor		

Source: Adapted from Harrison, Weisman, & Zornado (2017, p. 140).

agency incident report writing policy, supervisory requirements, and mandates of the local courts and prosecutor's office.

Battery

On the above date and time, I was escorting Nurse Smith for med pass on Unit 2. We went into D block for lockdown meds. When going up the left side stairs, I could see inmate Jones, John 123456 pacing in his Cell 16. He does not receive meds, since I could see he was up and alert I didn't get any closer for a HUS check. As I approached Cell 15, I observed Nurse Smith walking up to his cell. I witnessed inmate Jones reach out of his cell and grab Nurse Smith. She jumped back and looked very startled. I immediately removed her from the block. She stated he grabbed me by the shoulder and neck area. Nurse Smith has a visible red mark to her clavicle area. I then escorted her to the clinic and had her seen by clinical staff.

Theft

Offender explained that when he walked on the pod, he was told his assigned cell was 210, he was attacked by several offenders, where he was robbed. Offender explained that he had the following items taken from him $250 worth of canteen, $60 worth of hygiene, two pair of shoes.

Questions for Discussion

1. As a reader, does the narrative answer all of your questions about what happened?
2. What impressions did you form about the writer, the supervisor who approved the report, and the agency as a whole?
3. If you wrote this narrative, what details would you recall about your investigation one year later if you were called to testify?
4. How much time would it take to write a narrative like the ones above? How would you convince a jury or judge that you completed a thorough and detailed investigation, but spent only 5 or 10 minutes writing the report?

Exercise 4.1

Select a narrative from the examples above. Without reading the suggested revisions below, make a list of errors that should be corrected to improve the writing. Next, in your own words, revise the narrative focusing on improving the errors identified in the list you created. When you are finished, ask another student to review your work and offer constructive criticism.

The following revisions represent far superior reports. Each of these narratives took just 5 minutes to write.

Revised Battery

On 03/05/2019, I escorted Nurse Smith for medication distribution to inmates in Unit 2. While in Unit D, I saw inmate John Jones, inmate number 23587, pacing in his cell, Cell 16. Jones does not receive medication. As I approached Cell 15, I saw Smith walking up to Cell 16. I saw Jones reach out of his cell and grab Smith. She jumped back and looked very startled. I immediately escorted Smith out of Unit D. Smith said Jones grabbed her by the shoulder and neck. I saw a red mark in the area of Smith's clavicle. I then escorted her to the clinic to be treated by clinical staff.

There was no indication of serious injuries at the time of this report. Nurse White and Dr. Allen treated Smith at the clinic. Smith said she did not want to press charges. Jones was moved from D block, Cell 16, and placed in segregation pending an administrative discipline review.

Revised Theft

At about 1100 hours on 03/05/2019, I met with Inmate Gonzalez in the interview room of Pod D. Gonzalez stated that at about 1600 hours on 03/04/2019, Inmate Williams stole $250 dollars in canteen funds from him. Gonzalez said Williams followed him into his cell, Pod D, Cell 16; held him against the cell wall; and took his canteen card. He said about 10 inmates stood outside the cell so he could not seek help from staff. Williams told Gonzalez he would be physically harmed by "his people" if Gonzalez reported the incident to staff. Gonzalez said he was not physically injured during the incident.

At about 1500 hours on 03/05/2019, Pod D was placed on lockdown so that all cells could be searched. Officer Green assisted with the search and searched Cell 12, which Williams is assigned to. During the search of Cell 12, Green discovered Gonzalez's canteen card hidden inside a small stack of letter paper. No other contraband items were found in Cell 12 during the search. Williams was moved to segregation pending further investigation.

Gonzalez refused to sign a written statement. Photos of Cell 12 and Gonzalez's canteen card were submitted as evidence.

Questions for Discussion

Select one of the revised narratives and respond to the following questions:

1. Is this narrative organized, cohesive, informative, and persuasive?
2. As a reader, does it answer all of your questions about what happened?
3. What impressions did you form about the writer, the supervisor who approved the report, and the agency as a whole?
4. If you wrote this report, what details would you recall about your investigation 1 year later if you were called to testify?
5. How much time would it take to write a narrative like the one above? Could you easily convince a jury or judge that you took the time to complete a thorough and detailed investigation of this case? Why?

Source: UFS Distributed by Universal Ulick for UFS (2016). Retrieved from: https://i.pinimg.com/736x/eb/46/7d/eb467db7bdc1e397bce15654dc4070c6--writers-write-writing-humor.jpg

Disciplinary Reports

When an inmate violates institutional administrative rules or inmate Rules of Conduct, a corrections officer may write a disciplinary report. Depending on facility policy, some cases may warrant a verbal warning or written warning before the officer files a written disciplinary report. According to the California Board of State and Community Corrections (n.d.), disciplinary reports are used to document inmate behavior, justify administration segregation, provide information for classification, and as a cause of action for disciplinary hearings (p. 9). A sample disciplinary report is provided in Figure 4.1.

Disciplinary reports may document an inmate who possesses contraband (phone, drugs, etc.), acts violently, or assaults an inmate or officer. Olson (2016) observed that prison overcrowding, high inmate-to-staff ratios, and extensive rules often contribute to violations that require inmate discipline (p. 760). In the News 4.2 illustrates the various institutional causes for disciplinary action and the types of infractions that often require a disciplinary report.

When writing a disciplinary report, officers should follow the guidelines provided earlier in this chapter on writing an incident narrative. Some agencies may use a separate inmate disciplinary report, such as the one illustrated in Figure 4.2. But not all agencies do this. Since the disciplinary report closely mirrors an incident report, some agencies use the incident report form to document inmate misconduct. As with an incident report, the disciplinary report must be detailed and well written in all respects.

In the News 4.2

Disciplinary reports remain high as Davison County Jail population rises

In a jail becoming more crowded, disciplinary actions remain near historic highs.

In the first four months of the year, Davison County Jail staff have written 41 disciplinary reports, which range from disorderly conduct to possession of contraband such as prescription medications. Infractions are broken down into different classes. Violent and serious actions—including fighting, bribery and setting fires—are Class A offenses that result in immediate lockdown. Class B offenses, such as possessing drugs or tattooing someone, may also result in immediate lockdown. Minor violations include disrespecting staff and littering.

Staff can then take one of five actions. First is a verbal or written warning. Second, reserved for inmates released for work or Alcoholics Anonymous treatment, is a loss of participation in the program. (Shama, 2017)

Figure 4.1 is an example of a simple disciplinary report. This type of form might be used for nonviolent, administrative charges that do not involve inmate/inmate or inmate/officer confrontation, injuries, property damage, or loss of property.

Figure 4.2 allows for more detail than the previous example. The reporting officer is able to record evidence collected, and the supervisor can document action taken as a result of the violation. Note Part III, used to document witnesses interviewed.

Evidence Reports

The evidence report is used to document any item that has been seized by an officer or has evidentiary value. The report also establishes a chain of custody so that seized items can be presented in court. Advances in the technology available to criminal justice agencies have expanded the scope of items of evidentiary value to include video and audio recorded on cell phones, body cameras, housing unit cameras located in adult and juvenile detention facilities, courtroom cameras, and surveillance cameras. This report is often an addendum to the incident report. The format and style of these forms varies greatly from one agency to another.

Officers regularly conduct searches of cells and prisoners for a variety of reasons. Routine cell shakedowns are performed to find items of contraband such as drugs, weapons, cell phones, and other items prohibited by jail policy. Even when contraband isn't discovered, these searches send a message to inmates that the prison is intent on locating these items and charging prisoners with their possession.

The Fourth Amendment of the U.S. Constitution protects citizens from unreasonable government searches and seizures. With some exceptions, searches of a person, their effects, and their home require a search warrant based upon probable cause and signed by the judge. One such exception relates to a prisoner's right to privacy and the application of the Fourth Amendment requirements to prison cells, prison grounds, and prisoners.

Figure 4.1 Sample Inmate Disciplinary Warning Report

SOP 209.01
Attachment 12
11/6/17

Offender ____________________ ID Number ____________________

Charge(s) ____________________

______ Date ______ Time of Offense ______ Signature of Reporting Official

Factual Statement: ____________________

Sanctions: (Circle One)
Verbal Reprimand Counselor Referral Writing Assignment (500 words)

Extra Duty: ____________________

Other: ____________________

Reviewed and signed by the appropriate Supervisor ____________________

Supervisor Comments: ____________________

Retention Schedule: Upon completion, this form shall become part of the offender's institutional file, except for those overturned or dismissed, and shall be kept according to the official records retention schedule for institutional files.

Available at https://www.powerdms.com/public/GADOC/documents/240076.

Figure 4.2 Sample Inmate Disciplinary Report

State of Vermont Department of Corrections
Inmate Disciplinary Report

Part I - Completed by Reporting Officer

Facility:

Docket number:

Inmate name:

DOB: PID #

Living assignment:

Date/Time of incident:

Location of incident:

☐ Check if the witness(es) is/are confidential. If so, do not list.

Witnesses:

Minor Violation:

Major Violation:

Evidence:

Signature of Reporting Officer:

Delivered by:

Initials & Date/Time of delivery

Part II - Completed by Shift Supervisor

Was the inmate segregated as a result of the charged violation? ◯ Yes ◯ No Date segregated:

If Yes, the Notice of Hearing must be delivered within three (3) business days, the hearing held within four (4) business days.

Is the inmate SFI? ◯ Yes ◯ No If Yes, refer inmate to a QMHP for assessment before hearing is held.

Name of QMHP performing assessment:

If SFI and moved to segregation, were contraindications checked before being moved? ◯ Yes ◯ No

Did a Physician approve this housing? ◯ Yes ◯ No Name of approving Physician:

Supervisor signature:

Employee assigned as Investigator:

Part III - Completed by Investigating Officer

Did you interview confidential informants? ◯ Yes ◯ No

If Yes, see *Confidential Informant Form* for guidance.

Did you interview relevant witnesses? ◯ Yes ◯ No

Briefly explain:

Did you interview the inmate? ◯ Yes ◯ No

Briefly explain:

Did you compile available documentary evidence and statements of witnesses? ◯ Yes ◯ No

Briefly explain:

Investigating Officer's recommendation:

☐ Refer for resolution ☐ Do not refer for resolution

☐ Modify violation to:

Investigating Officer's signature:

Note: If the inmate is SFI by evidence of Part II, an assessment report by the QMHP must accompany this form to the Hearing Officer prior to the hearing.

Distribution: Hearing packet, Offender *May 2012*

Available at http://doc.vermont.gov/about/policies/rpd/index-of-department-of-corrections-forms/correctional-services-301-550/401-500-programs-security-and-supervision/inmate-disciplinary-report-form/view.

Goring (1984) notes "that the Fourth Amendment does not protect prisoners from searches of their personal property by correctional officers" (p. 609). The U.S. Supreme Court ruled in *Lanza v. New York* (1962) that the Fourth Amendment does not protect prison cells or prison property. Additionally, the court decided that a prisoner has no expectation of privacy within a prison generally or within a prison cell (*Hudson v. Palmer*, 1984). Subsequently, prisoners have no Fourth Amendment protections from search and seizure. As such, corrections officers and other government officials are authorized to search prisoners, their cells, and their property without the requirement for obtaining a search warrant prior to conducting the search.

Property items can be almost anything of evidence or monetary value: contraband, found stolen items, any item that creates a link between a suspect and a crime, cash, drugs, firearms, and much more. The evidence report form is a legal document that keeps a record of the collection, transportation, storage, chain of custody, and release of any item that comes into custody. Seized items are stored in a secure evidence room until they can be legally returned to the owner, destroyed, or auctioned as unclaimed property.

Officers must accurately describe any items that have been collected. An accurate description of evidence is vital to the successful prosecution of a case. Officers must be detailed yet cautious in describing drugs, jewelry, money, and other valuables.

Drugs

Illegal and prescription drugs are exceedingly popular and varied in prison and jail society. As such, officers are often confronted with the task of describing pills, powders, capsules, and more. An officer may recognize commonly seized drugs such as cocaine or cannabis. Many drugs can be quickly identified with a chemical field presumption test kit. But for submission and description purposes, any account of these items should be purposely generic since a substance's identity cannot be certain without a lab or expert analysis.

When describing drugs, officers should use the following terminology:

Powder cocaine—unknown white powder, suspected cocaine

Crack cocaine—unknown substance, suspected crack cocaine

Cannabis—unknown green leafy substance, suspected cannabis

Heroin—unknown (color) powder, suspected heroin

Prescription pill or capsule—unknown (color) pill (list any markings such as manufacturer, numbers, and cross score)

Money

Money must be counted accurately. All monies should be recounted several times with at least one other person present to verify the amount. In recording money on the evidence form, the officer should list the total amount, the nationality of the funds, and the number of each denomination. Many agencies require video recording cash seizures and submitting the recording as evidence as well. Cash should be submitted immediately to the agency evidence section to avoid any accusations of impropriety.

Example:

> $1,000 U.S. currency in the following denominations: five $100 bills, four $50 bills, and fifteen $20 bills.

Jewelry

Jewelry is often collected from an inmate during the intake process. Like describing narcotics, the prevalence, variety, and value of jewelry demands caution when it comes time to list items on an evidence form. Jewelry manufacturers are particularly adept at creating imitation jewelry that appears surprisingly authentic. Some synthetic stones, in fact, cannot be distinguished from their authentic counterparts without the aid of a trained jeweler or gemologist.

Jewelry should be described based on its appearance. When describing a woman's wedding band, for example, one should focus on the color and shape of the stone and ring rather than describing it as a diamond in a gold band. Officers should be equally cautious when describing items that carry a brand name since many counterfeiters have produced copies that are very difficult to distinguish from the real thing. A corrections officer is not a professional jeweler.

Here are some suggestions for describing jewelry and watches.

Instead of a diamond ring, write:

1. One woman's ring with a gold-colored band containing a single round clear-colored stone.
2. One woman's ring with a silver-colored band and a single round clear-colored stone surrounded by eight smaller round, blue-colored stones.

Instead of a Rolex watch, write:

1. One man's wristwatch with a round, blue-colored face and a silver-and-gold-colored wristband.
2. One man's wristwatch with a square, tan-colored face and a wristband.

Instead of a gold chain, write:

1. A woman's neck chain, 18 inches long, gold colored.
2. A man's neck chain, 24 inches long, gold colored, with a round medallion, also gold colored.

Use of Force Reports

It often becomes necessary for corrections officers to use force in order to protect themselves and others. According to the American Correctional Association Public Policy (2017) Use of Force report, force includes the use of restraints for other than routine transportation and movement, chemical agents, electronic devices, and weapons (p. 25). Less lethal use of force incidents are usually spontaneous events that occur in a housing unit between an officer and a single inmate (Hepburn, Griffin, & Petrocelli, 1997). The use of lethal force is much rarer and typically to prevent an escape or control a riot (Hepburn et al., 1997).

Most corrections agencies regulate the use of force through agency policy. A typical use of force policy includes details on subject resistance levels and officer response levels. These levels are outlined in Table 4.4. When writing a use of force report, it is particularly important for the officer to use the agency's use of force policy language to describe the inmate's behavior and the officer's response. By mirroring the policy language, the writer enables the audience to easily determine the officer applied an appropriate level of force given the inmate's conduct. Details that should be included in the use of force report are listed in Table 4.5.

Table 4.4 Use of Force Resistance and Response Levels

Inmate Resistance Level	Officer Response Level
Verbal The inmate uses profanity or hostile language toward the officer.	**Presence** The officer establishes compliance through the use of the badge and uniform, verbal commands, and body language.
Passive resistance	Physical contact
Active resistance	Physical control
Serious resistance	Use of less lethal weapons
Deadly resistance	Deadly force

Source: Adapted from Webb (2011).

Table 4.5 Common Details to Be Included in the Use of Force Report

Event	Use of Force	Post Event
Inmate name, history, and classification	Weapon used	Details of a search of the area and any evidence discovered
Location of event	Whether the weapon was effective in gaining control	Notification of a supervisor
Physical threat posed by the inmate	Reasons for any increased use of force or additional weapons used	
Number of inmates involved	The names of assisting officers and/or witnesses	
Any efforts made to control the incident		
Description of officer or inmate injuries and details of medical treatment		

Source: Adapted from Deschutes County Adult Jail (2015).

In many agencies, policy requires an officer to complete the use of force report prior to end of the shift anytime physical force is used (Deschutes County Adult Jail, 2015; Minnesota Department of Corrections, 2018; Santa Clara County Sheriff's Office, 2017).

Conclusion

Writing well requires a process of planning, writing, and editing. Whether putting pen to paper or writing electronically, producing the best written work cannot be accomplished by simply writing alone. The written report is where an officer becomes a storyteller and engages the audience. The report should be written chronologically in narrative format to tell a story using descriptive words. Officers should follow general writing guidelines, eliminate slang and jargon and emotion, and answer all appropriate interrogatives. All writing must be written in standard English and error free. Finally, a well-written document requires editing. Writers should edit every written document at the word and sentence level as well as globally. Following these guidelines will help writers produce quality writing that reflects positively on themselves and the agency.

QUESTIONS FOR CONSIDERATION

1. Why is style an important aspect of writing in criminal justice? Include a discussion of narrative and descriptive writing and tone.
2. Define point of view. What are first person and third person points of view. What is the preferred point of view (if agency policy permits)?
3. What is jargon? List three to five examples and alternative words that are easier for the audience to understand.
4. Define the audience for corrections reports and the importance of writing for this audience.
5. Partner with a student and review the section on describing jewelry. In narrative form, describe the student's jewelry as an officer would for an evidence report.

CHAPTER

5

Other Documents:

Memos, Letters, Emails, Cover Letters, and Resumes

Criminal justice, like most professions, requires a lot of writing. As has been repeated many times in this book, being able to write skillfully and in a business-like manner is very important in establishing confident relationships and creating a positive image for agencies and their employees. Aside from writing job-related reports used to process criminal and civil cases, criminal justice professionals are tasked with business writing, such as memos, letters, and emails. All of these require professionalism, a business tone, proper formatting, and good English grammar. Additionally, criminal justice professionals engage in cover letter and resume writing to acquire their positions in the first place.

This chapter focuses on some universal rules and guidelines for writing various business documents and reports used by criminal justice professionals. Memos, letters, emails, and resumes will be discussed, in general.

Writing Business-Related Documents

Criminal justice professionals are required to write a number of various types of documents. The skills needed to write these documents require criminal justice professionals to be proficient in business or professional writing. Business writing is a type of professional communication. It is often called business communication and is used to convey information within and outside of agencies to specific audiences (Nordquist, 2018). The goal of business writing is to provide information quickly and clearly to the audience. Business writing is not a skill that people are born with, but it can be cultivated over time and with practice (Garner, 2013).

Business writing consists of both a style and a format or structure. Documents written in a professional style should accomplish a number of goals (Nordquist, 2018):

1. Convey information and/or deliver news—the document should communicate information in a clear and concise manner to the internal or external audience.
2. Direct an action and explain or justify the action—the document should tell the audience what they should do and why they should do it.
3. Influence others to take action—the document should encourage others to take the action requested or to change a policy, procedure, or in the case of for-profit companies, adopt a particular product or service.

Memos, letters, and emails are excellent choices for business writing because they allow the writer to accomplish these goals. Along with the style of writing, business writing mostly follows standard formatting rules.

In general, business documents all look the same because standard formats are used in writing them. Using headings, dates, addresses, salutations, purpose paragraphs, and closing paragraphs are all considered part of the standard format in professional writing (Nordquist, 2018). Left justification, single spacing, and avoiding jargon are also generally accepted practices. Paragraphs are not indented in these documents. Instead adding a space between the paragraphs is sufficient for separating ideas and topics. Using everyday words, active verbs, and a conservative amount of contractions is also acceptable in formal professional writing (Nordquist, 2018). Along with a standard typeface font, like Times New Roman, writers rely on bullets, graphs, tables, and boldface and italics when needing to emphasize important points (Gale, 2014).

Work-related writing can include memos, letters, emails, and resumes. The following sections will discuss the various types of professional documents one is likely to write when working in criminal justice.

Memos

Memos are often considered an informal means of communication; however, memos are professional documents and are used to convey very important policy or procedure information to employees. Thus, knowing how to properly write a memo and what to include in a memo is an important skill for professionals. Memos usually have eight main sections: heading, opening, context, task, summary, discussion, closing, and attachments, if necessary (Purdue OWL, 2018c). Although the memo can follow that format, the writer may place the sections in any order as long as he or she pays close attention to the readability of the memo (Purdue OWL, 2018c). In other words, the writer should write the memo in whatever order makes the most sense and is easiest to read. An example of a memo is provided in Figure 5.1.

Components of a Memo

The heading of a memo is found in list form and provides the name and title of the person to whom the memo is written, the name and title of the person sending the memo, the date the memo is written, and the subject of the memo. Because the memo is a formal means to communicate with those holding positions higher or lower than the sender of the memo, the names and titles should be written formally, and the subject should be concise but specific so those reading the memo understand its purpose (Purdue OWL, 2018c).

The opening of the memo is found in the first paragraph and includes a specific statement identifying the purpose, context, and assignment or task associated with the memo. In this paragraph, the writer of the memo provides a brief overview of what the memo is about and expresses the importance of reading the memo in full (Purdue OWL, 2018c). Additionally, the opening of the memo sets the tone for the remainder of the information found in the document. The opening is typically no more than one paragraph (i.e., a minimum of three sentences; Purdue OWL, 2018c).

Figure 5.1 Sample Memo

To: Ruby Smith, Assistant Supervisor, Division of Child and Family Services
From: Lamonte Jones, Chief, Juvenile Probation and Family Court Services
Date: January 14, 2018
Subject: Family Reunification and Termination Act of 2018 and Case Review Procedures

The purpose of this memo is to explain delayed decision making for protective custody cases that may result in a termination of parental rights in lieu of reunification.

Changes are being implemented to the termination of parental rights policies, per the federal Family Reunification and Termination Act of 2018 (81 USCS § 11907). The new Act requires that all parenting reunification plans provide a minimum of 13 months of reunification activities, to include visitations, individual and family counseling, parenting classes, and one additional status hearing in front of the judge, prior to a decision on terminating parental rights.

As a result of these mandates, all termination of parental rights decisions made by the Permanency Planning Task Force will be delayed until after the 14th month of protective custody. Existing cases that have already passed the 14th month of protective custody will undergo review for termination of parental rights beginning on or about June 30, 2018. Existing cases that have not reached the 14th month of protective custody will be reviewed for compliance with the reunification requirements found in the Act beginning on or about June 30, 2018.

To prepare for the upcoming implementation of the directives, please review with all child protective services case workers and the Permanency Planning Task Force the Parenting Reunification and Termination of Parental Rights Act of 2018 (81 USCS § 11907). In addition, please prepare the following information for discussion at the Director's business meeting on April 30, 2018.

1. A list of existing protective custody cases that are 14 months or older including services already offered in each case and deficiencies in services based on the new mandates
2. A list of existing protective custody cases that are 13 months or less including services already offered in each case and deficiencies in services based on the new mandates

If there is anything I can do to assist with these tasks or to answer questions you or your subordinates may have, please let me know. I have full confidence that our agency will come into compliance with the mandates quickly and continue the high level of service our clients expect. Thank you in advance for your continued commitment to our mission.

The context of the memo provides the policy, procedure, or experience that is being solved by the memo. For example, the chief probation officer may write a memo to his or her subordinates explaining the new procedure for dismissing cases that successfully complete drug court. In the context of the memo, the writer may explain the previous task or method (how drug court cases were dismissed in the past) and then state the new task or method (the new document, dismissal procedure, or form to be filed) to be used moving forward. Often, the context of the memo can be fully clarified in one or two sentences (Purdue OWL, 2018c).

The task of the memo builds upon the context section by describing what is being done to comply with the policy, implement the new procedure, or solve the problem (Purdue OWL, 2018c). If an action is being requested by an administrator to lower level employees, such as corrections officers being asked to wear body cameras, the task section provides the space to make this request. If the memo writer is asking an administrator to make a change, the task section also provides this opportunity. For example, a line-staff member, like a correctional officer, may write a memo to the shift captain asking him or her to change the way inmate telephone calls are handled to better accommodate the lines that form by the phones. Changing the line structure may increase security and decrease stress and potential arguments among inmates. This would be an important point for the line-staff member to add into the memo.

The summary of the memo is optional when compared to the other sections described. If the memo is more than one page, the summary plays an important role in restating the key information found in the memo. However, if the memo is brief, the summary may not be necessary. The summary may be accomplished in a single sentence, depending on its need and purpose. Lastly, the summary allows for the writer to provide reference and source information they may have used in the memo (Purdue OWL, 2018c).

It is in the discussion of the memo that the writer provides the details that support the requests for change. The discussion section should provide the most vital information first, followed by secondary information that supports the recommendations. It is in the discussion that research or factual arguments may be introduced, with the strongest arguments coming first followed by weaker arguments (if there are any; Purdue OWL, 2018c).

The closing of the memo should provide the reader an opportunity for further discussion and clarity. The closing should be considerate of the new actions the writer is asking someone to make or to consider (Purdue OWL, 2018c). Finally, any attachments needed to support the information in the memo can be stapled or paperclipped to the memo. The writer should refer to these attachments somewhere in the framework of the memo (Purdue OWL, 2018c).

Letters

Everyone is flooded with letters from businesses, alumni associations, marketing firms, and charities requesting donations. Many times, these letters are quickly disposed of in the closest trash can; however, letters are a very important form of communication for these groups. According to The Business Communication (2018), letters are used to sell products, make inquiries about services, build community relationships, increase goodwill, and perform many other functions. Letters are also used as covers (called cover letters) for resumes and applications for jobs. In criminal justice, letters are used to build relationships, communicate confidential and legal information, and notify individuals of procedures, processes, and official expectations. Criminal justice letters are sources of proof for courts and can maintain secrecy regarding legal issues and concerns (The Business Communication, 2018).

Letters in criminal justice follow the same general format described for all business communication. They are single spaced using a block font, like Times New Roman, and they use a formal tone without relying on jargon. Criminal justice letters have multiple components, just as memos, and include headings, the recipient's address, salutations, the body of the letter, the closing, and the signature line. The letters can also refer to and include attachments, if needed. Common attachments, also known as enclosures, to a business letter in criminal justice may include court orders, requests to produce documents to other parties, and/or copies of warrants, fines, or other court business. Criminal justice letters are written on agency stationery, which identifies them as a formal document and form of communication from the court or another organization.

Components of a Letter

The heading of a business letter includes the writer's name, title, address, phone number, fax number, and email address (Doyle, 2018a). If the writer is communicating on behalf of an organization or business, the writer will use the company's address as their location. The date appears after the writer's contact information. There is a double space between the date and the recipient's information (as noted in the business letter example in Figure 5.2).

Immediately following the date identifying when the letter is written is the recipient's information. The recipient's information includes the formal name and title followed by his or her address (Doyle, 2018a). If the recipient's name is not known, the sender may use a title, like President, Vice President, or Director of Communications, and the primary address of the company. The sender will double space between the header and the recipient's information and then directly following the recipient's information include a double space again. The recipient's information is followed by the salutation.

The salutation is the greeting of the letter (Doyle, 2018a). It is always formal and begins with Dear followed by the person's name. If the gender of the person is known, the sender can put Mr., Mrs., Miss, or Ms. and the last name of the receiver after Dear. For example, Dear Mr. Jones. However, if the gender of the recipient is unknown or unclear, the sender can use both the first and last name of the recipient in the salutation. If there is a formal title for the receiver, such as Officer or Captain, the sender can also use the title in the salutation. Examples of this include Dear Officer Mack or Dear Cpt. Smith. If the name of the recipient is not known, the sender can write "To Whom It May Concern" as the salutation. This is the most formal, yet generic, salutation for unknown recipients. The salutation should be punctuated with a comma or colon depending on the salutation used and the formality of the letter. More formal letters require colons after the salutation.

The body of the letter begins after a double space after the salutation. It is left justified and single spaced. Double spaces should be used between paragraphs. The body of the letter contains the nuts and bolts of the information being provided by the sender. It states the reason for the letter and provides a more detailed explanation of what is expected from the receiver, what the receiver may need to say or do, whom he or she may need to contact, and/or information about products, services, and ways to access each (Doyle, 2018a). For example, if a probation officer is informing a probationer to seek anger management classes, probation officer would provide

Figure 5.2 Sample Official Letter

Fairview County Probation Department
113 N. Oak Dr.
Lakeland, MN 47890
978-356-1110
Email: mjones@fairviewcounty.gov

Mark Jones
Fairview County Probation Department
113 N. Oak Dr.
Lakeland, MN 47890

September 4, 2017

Margaret Smith
1337 Pine St.
Lakeland, MN 47890

Dear Ms. Smith,

Per our phone conversation I am attaching a copy of the YCUSA Program shoplifting diversion schedule. As you are aware, you have been court ordered to attend and complete a shoplifting diversion course within the next six weeks.

To schedule your course please contact Rhonda Jacobs at the YCUSA Program by phone at 978-344-0765 or by email at rjacobs@ycusa.org. Once you have scheduled your course please provide the date and time you plan to attend to my office. A completion certificate will be provided to me for your file by YCUSA once you have successfully completed the class.

If you have additional questions or concerns please let me know. If I can be of assistance to you in the future please do not hesitate to reach out.

Sincerely,

Mark Jones

Mark Jones
Fairview County Probation Department

Cc: File

Enclosures

the name, address, and phone number of the organization supplying the class in the body of the letter. The probation officer would also tell the probationer the name of the contact person at the organization and the dates he or she is to appear for the first class. The body of the letter should be formal and end with a double space prior to the close of the letter.

The final two components of an official letter are the closing and the signature line. The closing of the letter is a short statement such as "Thank you" or "Sincerely" that signifies the letter is ending (Doyle, 2018a). The first word in the closing statement is capitalized and the closing is followed by a comma. There are usually four spaces between the closing statement and the signature line of the letter. The signature line includes the first and last name and title of the sender of the letter, for example, Susan Jones, Media Communications Specialist Benning County Corrections Center. Additionally, the sender signs, using cursive writing, their first and last name in the four spaces provided between the closing and signature lines.

If necessary, and enclosures are attached, a double space follows the signature line and then the word "Enclosures." If no attachments are included, this word will not appear on the letter. Finally, if the letter is being shared with another party, the sender will put "cc:" (copy circulation) and identify the party receiving a copy of the letter. If this is noted, the receiver will know where else the letter is located and anyone else aware of the contents of the letter. An example of this is also provided in Figure 5.2, which shows the format of a formal letter.

Emails

Emails are used to communicate formally and informally. When emailing friends and family, one may use an informal tone that includes emojis and slang as well as a personal email address through Yahoo.com or Hotmail.com. The email may include incomplete sentences, lots of exclamation points, and

"I got your email. Was it encrypted or is your spelling *that* bad?"

Source: @ Mike Baldwin; www.cartoonstock.com.

misspellings. Conversely, when writing in one's profession, emails should be written in a formal tone and be sent through the agency's email system using a professional email address. The content of the email should be free from grammar errors and should be left justified. There should be limited use of slang, jargon, and no emojis.

Components of an Email

The layout of a formal email is similar to that of an official letter, with the exception of the header. Unlike a letter, a prescribed header is not necessary. Instead of providing an official header with the sender's name, title, and address at the top of the email, the sender can place this information below the signature line. Additionally, day, time, or year does not need to be placed at the top of an email. Since an email system, like Yahoo, Gmail, or some other business software system, generally includes the sender's name, recipient's name, email addresses for both, and date in the email sending system, the writer does not need to provide this information in a formal way at the top of the body of the email. Instead, the email can just begin with the salutation and body paragraph. The topic of the email should be included in the subject line of the email. An email address box will automatically look like the example in Box 5.1.

Box 5.1

From: Janice Long <jlong@marioncountyprobation.gov>

To: Ryan Langston <rlangston@marioncountyprobation.gov>

Thu., 7/15/2018 4:19 PM

Subject: Draft of Probation Contract

If an individual is circulating a copy of the email to others, their names will appear at the top of the email in the address box as well, even if they are not actually addressed by name in the salutation of the email. In this case, the email will appear as noted in Box 5.2.

Box 5.2

From: Janice Long <jlong@marioncountyprobation.gov>

To: Ryan Langston <rlangston@marioncountyprobation.gov>

Cc: Randall Allen <rallen@marioncountyprobation.gov>

Thu., 7/15/2018 4:19 PM

Subject: Draft of Probation Contract

There is the option for a sender to blind copy circulate someone in an email (known as bcc). If this occurs, the recipient will not know this has transpired; although, the sender of the email will see the blind-copied person's name and email address in their address line (as shown in Box 5.3). It is important to always remain professional and formal in emails since one may not know who is reading the final product.

Box 5.3

From: Janice Long <jlong@marioncountyprobation.gov>

To: Ryan Langston <rlangston@marioncountyprobation.gov>

Cc: Randall Allen <rallen@marioncountyprobation.gov>

Bcc: Stan Cox <scox@marioncountyprobation.gov>

Thu., 7/15/2018 4:19 PM

Subject: Draft of Probation Contract

An important point to remember is that emails, like letters, can be used as evidence in court and as formal means of notification, in most states. Signature lines and signature blocks on emails have been considered legitimate authentication indicators by many state courts, and individuals can testify to the authentication of emails. Even deleted emails can be found again on Internet servers and used as court evidence. Additionally, emails can be traced from computers across Internet servers, so their authentication can be legitimized. With this said, what one sends in both formal and informal emails should not be considered private. Email is a formal means of communication, regardless of the tone of the email or from where the email is sent, and is a legally recognized way to communicate in criminal justice.

Exercise 5.1

Write a formal email and an informal email. In your opinion, when is it appropriate to send an informal email to a colleague at work?

Like emails, most people consider social media an informal means of communication. However, it is used more and more by criminal justice professionals to convey information. Just like emails, postings on social media can also be used in court and as official forms of communication. Consequently, this chapter would be remiss if postings on social media were also not discussed.

Anything posted on the Internet is a reflection on an individual and, potentially, on the company or agency employing that person. Accordingly, some companies monitor social media postings by their employees, and/or forbid use of the Internet and social media while employees are at work. Checking social media sites for past postings and comments is a common practice during the hiring process. CareerBuilder (2017) reported that more than 70% of companies use social media to screen candidates before hiring them, an increase of 50% since 2006, and over a third of companies have reprimanded or fired individuals for inappropriate comments posted on social media. Thus, posting pictures of weekend drinking habits or making comments about clients or supervisors may not bode well in a job search or once employed in criminal justice.

For the most part, employees in criminal justice are forbidden to post formal messages to individual supervisors, subordinates, clients, or offenders on social media sites. They are, instead, required to rely on more formal means of communication, like letters and emails. Nearly all criminal justice agencies hire media experts to handle official communications from their agencies. These individuals are trained in speaking with the media, making public posts on social media sites, and handling questions or concerns from citizens.

Cover Letters and Resumes

To get a job in the first place usually requires a cover letter and resume. This means that everyone needs to know how to write these two documents. An Internet search for both provides a plethora of information and formatting guidelines. The simplest of these rules, though, are to provide as much information as possible about one's skills and qualifications; to proofread the work and fix all errors; to properly format; to personalize the correspondence with names, titles, and company names of the recipients; and to follow the instructions provided by the business to apply for the wanted position (Writing Center of Wisconsin–Madison, 2018). Cover letters are considered the first impression from the candidate and, as such, should be formal and concise.

Components of a Cover Letter

A cover letter should follow the same business communication format for letters discussed earlier. It should be left justified, in a formal block 12-point font, written in formal tone with little jargon or slang, and be personalized to the person and company hiring for the job. A cover letter should be seen as the candidate's formal introduction and should provide the reason for the letter, relate his or her skills to the job's requirements, and request a meeting or discussion with the person interviewing applicants. A cover letter, like other forms of formal communication, should be written on crisp, clear, white paper and be error free.

A cover letter should include headings, salutations, a body, and a closing. It should also indicate that a resume or application, if required, is attached

(Doyle, 2018b). According to Doyle (2018b), a cover letter should include three key components:

1. A stated reason for the letter: I am applying for the position of correctional officer at Smithville Correctional Institution. I have attached my resume for your review.
2. Job skills and other qualifications that relate to the job description or job advertisement: I have worked as a security officer for McMurphee Security Company for more than 3 years and have experience in inmate transportation with Wilson Transportation. I also speak fluent Spanish and hold an associate degree in criminal justice.
3. Information on how you will follow up with the hiring manager and/or how you can be reached for an interview: I look forward to speaking with you about this position. I will call the Office of Human Resources to make sure my application is complete on Wednesday, June 2, 2018, *or* alternatively, I look forward to speaking with you about the position. If you need additional information, please contact me at 321-999-0101 or lalannam@hotmail.com.

The candidate should use the cover letter to demonstrate how he or she will add to the agency, not what the agency can do for him or her (Doyle, 2018b). Additionally, the cover letter allows the candidate to show professionalism and writing skills. The cover letter is the candidate's first, and sometimes only, chance to garner the attention of the person doing the hiring, so the cover letter should be taken seriously and checked and rechecked for crucial information.

Additionally, Gallo (2014) suggests the following when writing cover letters:

Do

- Have a strong opening statement that makes clear why you want the job and why you're right for it
- Be succinct—a hiring manager should be able to read it at a glance
- Share an accomplishment that shows you can address the challenges the employer faces

Don't

- Try to be funny—too often if falls flat
- Send a generic cover letter—customize each one for the specific job
- Go overboard with flattery—be professional and mature

Cover letters should distinguish a candidate from other job candidates but not seem fake or disingenuous by losing sight of why the candidate is applying for the position to begin with—because he or she really wants to work in this field or for this agency.

There is no need to crowd too much information on a cover letter. The cover letter should contain plenty of white space and only needs to provide three or four paragraphs, at most. Using perfumed paper or colored paper to print the cover letter is unnecessary and may actually be a distraction from the message the candidate is trying to send. Finally, the candidate should reply with a cover letter to a job advertisement in the method requested by the job advertisement. If the company asks for an emailed cover letter, then by all means one should email it. If the cover letter is requested to be hand-delivered or postal mailed, then the candidate should do that. In some cases, the job applicant may be asked to copy and paste the cover letter into an online application system. If this is the case, the candidate should still make sure the letter is formatted properly and is error free when pasted into the textbox. Along with the cover letter, a candidate may be asked to provide a resume.

Components of a Resume

Resumes are used for a variety of purposes. A person may create a resume to apply for a job, to apply for a raise or promotion, or for their annual employee evaluation. By far the most common reason a person creates a resume is to get an interview for a job (Purdue OWL, 2018d). A resume should be attached to a cover letter, if requested or required by the job advertisement. These two documents go together in the professional world.

A resume is used to present a person's skills and qualifications, background, and education for a job. A resume is not a letter, is not lengthy, and should be considered more of an outline that demonstrates a person's unique history and ability to do the job they are applying for. A resume contains essential contact information for the candidate. This is not in the form of a formal header, like in a formal letter, but is typically centered on the top of the page and simply lists the contact information (Purdue OWL, 2018d):

The candidate's full name

Address (permanent or temporary)

Phone (landline and cell phone, if applicable, and fax number)

Email address

Web address (if applicable)

To underscore the contact information, a candidate may choose to use a larger font for his or her name, to bold their name, and/or to use a line between the contact information and the additional information provided in the resume (Purdue OWL, 2018d). These tactics draw the interviewer's attention to the contact information. An example of this may appear as such:

LeLanna Michaels
1802 Live Oak Lane
Smithfield, Georgia 54678
Cell: 321-999-0101
Home: 321-995-9876
lmichaels@hotmail.com

Figure 5.3 Sample Resume

LeLanna Michaels
1802 Live Oak Lane
Smithfield, Georgia 54678
Cell: 321-999-0101
Home: 321-995-9876
Email: Lmichaels@hotmail.com

Objective:
To obtain an entry level position with Smithfield Correctional Institution that allows me to work with inmates and use my Spanish language skills.

Education:
- County Community College, Same County, MA Associate of Science in Criminal Justice, graduated May 2018

Work Experience:
- Wilson Transportation, *Driver* January 2017–Present
  Transport inmates to court, facilities, treatment centers, and halfway houses.
- McMurphee Security Company, *Security Officer* August 2013–January 2017

Secured buildings and other structures at the port, completed work logs, attended briefings and trainings, and collaborated with county and city police on investigations.

Awards and Honors:
- Dean's List, Fall 2017 and Spring 2018
- Honor Society for Criminal Justice, January 2018
- Employee of the Month, September 2017

Skills:
- Mandated State Police Certification, 2018
- Massachusetts Firearms Certification, 2014
- Georgia Firearms Certification, 2017–Present
- Fluent in Spanish
- Proficient in Microsoft Office Software
- Hardworking, dedicated, and punctual
- Great leadership skills

This format can be used on both the cover letter and the resume if they are presented together to the interviewer. This provides for uniformity across the two documents, presents a single professional package, and illustrates that they are from the same job applicant (Purdue OWL, 2018d).

Following the contact information, there should be subheadings that indicate the various parts of the resume. Although the subheadings may vary depending on what the purpose of the resume is (e.g., applying for a job, getting a raise or promotion, employee evaluation), a job candidate may highlight his or her education, achievements or awards, previous work experience, and skills. Candidates may also want to include an objective that identifies what they are trying to accomplish professionally. These areas are presented in Figure 5.3.

Companies often require candidates to provide references or names of individuals who can attest to the character, work experience, and background of a job applicant. At the end of a resume, a candidate can decide whether to provide references for his or her professional and personal character. If the candidate decides to provide references, he or she should indicate so by using the subheading "References" and then providing the names, titles, and professional contact information for the persons they have chosen to comment about their professional experience and character. If, however, a candidate decides not to provide references on the resume, the candidate can simply add "References Available Upon Request" to the bottom of the resume. This indicates to the hiring manager that there are individuals who can speak to the qualifications stated in the resume and signals that the hiring manager should contact the candidate if he or she would like to speak to the references. Candidates often use this choice if they do not want to have unnecessary phone calls made to their current or former supervisors and/or if they have not told their current supervisor that they are searching for a new position. Once the candidate is contacted for reference information, he or she can inform the current supervisor so he or she is alerted to the possibility of a telephone call. A candidate may also choose to use this phrase if he or she is still deciding who to ask as a character reference or if he or she needs time to contact the references before the agency does so.

Both resumes and cover letters introduce the candidate to the job interviewer. They should be used to highlight the most important and relevant education and skills a candidate has that relate to the position he or she is applying for. More detailed information on a candidate's experience can be provided once he or she is in person at the interview. When writing these documents, one should keep in mind that attention spans may be short, there may be lots of resumes to review, and the interviewer may not have a lot of time to review resumes before interviewing candidates, so keeping the resume and cover letter to a single page each is important. Longer resumes may only be acceptable if the candidate has had a lengthy career or has many special skills or qualifications related to the position. Candidates should ask themselves what it is about them that makes them uniquely qualified for the position and focus on that information in both the cover letter and resume.

CHAPTER SUMMARY

Criminal justice professionals spend much of their time writing. They are required to write professionally across many mediums, including memos, letters, emails, and, when applying for jobs or promotions, cover letters and resumes. Knowing how to write these documents and the standard formats expected in official communication is an essential skill and demonstrates a person's professionalism and abilities.

Memos and emails, although often considered informal means of communication, are legitimate communication documents and should always be treated as such. Writers of these documents should be conscientious of their purpose and the potential audience. They should also always keep in mind that these documents could be used by courts or by other criminal justice workers later to verify communications; the knowledge a person had about a policy, procedure, practice, or demand; and/or by the general public, if secured by the media or other sources. Letters, like those that may be sent from courts or probation offices, serve fundamental functions for the criminal justice system. Their tone and the information they contain may result in very serious consequences if the receiver chooses to ignore the message. In all of the above cases, memos, emails, and letters could follow a criminal or civil case from the beginning (arrest) to the end (prison or parole). Like with these more formal forms of communication, being aware of how one communicates on social media is also important.

Finally, to get a professional position in the first place, individuals have to write cover letters and resumes that stand out above other possibly suitable candidates. These documents must be able to gain the attention of hiring managers that may review many, many potential applicants. Cover letters and resumes should emphasize a person's unique qualifications for a position, while also demonstrating their professionalism and enthusiasm for the agency and job. Each one should be personalized for the position one is applying for and the company one is applying to.

To be proficient in any writing task, an individual needs to practice writing skills. A person should review templates and other examples and edit, edit, edit their own documents until just the right message is sent. A person must also constantly be careful when conveying a written message, as it is always a reflection on the writer.

QUESTIONS FOR CONSIDERATION

1. In what instances might a probation officer write a memo to the court? What about to a treatment provider? What message might the memo contain?
2. When writing a formal letter to an agency, what key elements should you include?
3. If you were a hiring manager, what errors would you look for in a cover letter to disqualify a candidate?
4. If you were to apply for a position as a corrections officer, what skills or qualifications would you highlight in your cover letter? What about on the resume?

CHAPTER 6

Academic Paper Formats:

What is APA Formatting?

College students are regularly asked to complete research papers in classes. The course instructor's directives for the paper probably require that students use academic formatting, most specifically American Psychological Association (APA) format. APA format is the accepted academic format for criminal justice writing. Students who become proficient in APA formatting while in college often find that they continue to use this approach when writing grants, reports, program evaluations, and other documents in their professional careers in criminal justice.

This chapter reviews the necessity for APA formatting in academic projects and discusses the types of manuscripts one is likely to see utilizing APA format, ethics and legal issues in writing and publishing, and plagiarism. Other formats, specifically the Modern Language Association (MLA) and the *Chicago Manual of Style (CMOS),* are briefly mentioned since students may be exposed to these styles as well.

Research, Publication, and the APA Style Rules

When someone decides to analyze data or complete a research project on a specific phenomenon, he or she becomes a researcher. That researcher's work or report may be relevant to the field of study where the phenomenon exists; thus, the researcher is expected to share the completed work with others. In doing so, the researcher expands the wealth of knowledge available to other scholars and practitioners and builds upon what is already known about a specific discipline and what may still need to be investigated. Their work provides new insight on a specific phenomenon and allows others to critically assess the research, expand it, complete future projects that do not repeat the same mistakes, and contribute something new to the field of study (APA, 2010). However, in order for the work to be completely communicated to others, there has to be a standard way of writing. This is where the APA format becomes important.

The American Psychological Association created the APA format in 1929 as a method whereby researchers could formally communicate scientific research results in publications (APA, 2010). The goal was to provide a set of procedures, or style rules, that codify the format of scientific research papers to simplify reading comprehension (VandenBos, 2010). The association has revised the APA style many times, and it often includes the input of psychologists, anthropologists, and business managers. The association also consults with other researchers in the social and behavioral sciences when determining updates to the style. The current format (7th edition) provided by the APA was developed in consultation with the Publication Manual Task Force, APA members at professional meetings, and APA boards and committees, which include students (APA, 2010). The style rules consist of instructions on formatting manuscripts, tables, figures, citations, and references, and the organization of papers as well as grammar and other basic information on the mechanics of writing. Some basic style guidelines from the APA manual are provided in Box 6.1 (APA, 2010).

Box 6.1

Basic Style Rules for APA Citations

APA requires resources to be cited both in the text of the document and at the end of a document, called a reference list. APA provides very extensive citation guidelines and rules for many types of sources in their style manual. Where they do not provide a style guideline for a source, students are encouraged to choose a sample style as similar to their source as they can. Although there are no standard citation rules for all sources, some basic guidelines are provided below:

In-Text Citations

- Writers should use past tense when referring to previous research completed by authors (e.g., Smith found).
- In-text citations should immediately follow the sentence where the information was paraphrased and/or quoted.
- Writers should follow the author–date style when citing sources in the text of a document (e.g., Smith, 2018).
- When directly quoting from a source, writers should provide the author's last name, date of publication, and a page number for the source where the information came from (e.g., Smith, 2017, p. 135).
- Writers should place the punctuation mark after the in-text citation.
- Writers should capitalize proper nouns, titles, and the first word after a colon or dash in an in-text citation.
- Writers should italicize the names of longer works if the work is used in the in-text citation instead of an author's name.
- Writers should put quotation marks around titles of journal articles, television shows, song titles, and articles from edited collections.
- Writers should use special style rules for quotations that are 40 or more words that include indenting the quotation by five spaces, omitting the quotation marks, starting the quotation on a new line, and placing the page number at the end of the quotation and after the punctuation mark.

The Reference List

- The reference list should appear at the end of the document and begin on a new page labeled "References" in the center of the page.
- Each resource cited in the document and in in-text citations should appear in the reference list.
- Writers should double-space references.
- If a reference is longer than one line, the second line should be indented five spaces as a hanging indentation.

- Writers should provide an author's last name first followed by the author's first and middle initials.
- All authors up to and including seven authors should be provided in the reference. Any authors after six should be indicated with an ellipsis except for the final author name, which should be included.
- Writers should alphabetize the references and use chronological order for multiple articles by the same author.
- Writers should italicize book titles, but not italicize, underline, or put quotation marks around titles of journal articles.
- Writers should provide the title in full.
- Writers should keep the punctuation and capitalization provided in a journal's name.
- Writers should capitalize the first letter in the first word of a title and subtitle, the first letter in the first word after a colon or dash, and proper nouns.

Source: Adapted from Purdue University (2018). The Purdue online writing lab. Retrieved from https://owl.purdue.edu/.

Why Use a Style Guide?

Often, students ask why there is an emphasis on writing style versus a simple focus on grammar and proper English. VandenBos (2010, p. xiv) stated,

> Uniform style helps us to cull articles quickly for key points and findings. Rules of style in scientific writing encourage full disclosure of essential information and allow us to dispense with minor distractions. Style helps us express the key elements of quantitative results, choose the graphic form that will best suit our analyses, report critical details of our research protocol, and describe individuals with accuracy and respect.

All of this clears the way for researchers to focus on the substance of their research, rather than the writing style (VandenBos, 2010).

Having a set of style rules also provides a formal system for journals, books, and other media to follow when publishing the work of researchers. Print media and digital media may require a researcher to format their work according to the APA style rules. In doing so, the work can be more easily read and reviewed by other scholars and those interested in the study. Box 6.2 provides general guidelines for information included in APA-formatted references.

Additionally, legitimizing the research is a requirement of the scientific research community. This usually involves a review of the manuscript by other experts familiar with the discipline who peer-review (or referee) the paper for theory, methods, data, and analysis. The reviewers assess the strength of the project in following the scientific protocol of research. They determine the strengths and weaknesses of the manuscript, which should also be provided by the researcher in the paper, and consider the rigor of the design, methodology, analysis, interpretation of the data, and reporting. Reviewers also verify the transparency of the study's details so that others

Box 6.2

General Information Included in APA-Formatted References

1. Author's name(s) written with last name first, followed by first initial and middle initial
2. Year of publication in parentheses
3. Title of book, article, paper, etc.
4. Journal name italicized (omitted if not a journal)
5. Volume number of the journal or edition of the book
6. Issue number of the journal in parentheses (omitted if not a journal)
7. Page numbers where article is printed within the journal (omitted if not a journal)
8. DOI number, unless there is no DOI, in which case the phrase "Retrieved from" and the URL of the website can be used
9. Geographical location (both city and state) and name of publishing company
10. End citation with a period

The APA style manual provides many examples of citations for databases, journals, unpublished papers, interviews, social media, and so forth. Students are encouraged to purchase the most up-to-date manual early in their academic careers and to refer to it frequently when writing academic papers.

may reproduce or extend the findings (National Institutes of Health, 2017). Reviews that end in positive appraisals are published, while those manuscripts that are reviewed negatively may need to be rewritten or revised to meet the standards of the scientific community. If reviewers conclude the manuscript has serious scientific, ethical, or legal flaws, the study may never be published.

Types of Publications

Journals

If a study is published, it may appear in a journal. Students are often familiar with journals because they do online and in-person library searches for articles on various topics when writing research papers. Journals come in a variety of formats (print and digital), as well as refereed and nonrefereed. A refereed journal will use the peer-reviewed practice described above, while a nonrefereed journal may publish articles that have only been reviewed by an editor or an editorial board who may or may not have knowledge and experience related to the reviewed article's topic. In this case, the article may be reviewed more for style and formatting than for scientific and academic validity.

Scholarly or refereed journals publish articles that are considered primary or original works and may consist of "empirical studies, literature reviews, theoretical articles, methodological articles, or case studies" (APA, 2010, p. 9). Empirical studies are original research projects that include secondary data analysis, testing hypotheses, and presentations of new data that may not have been presented in previous research studies. Literature reviews, which are most familiar to students, include synthesizing and critically evaluating previously published studies on a specific phenomenon (APA, 2010). Theoretical articles use existing publications to advance theory by reviewing the theory from development through time pointing out flaws and/or adding to or modifying the theory. Methodological articles present new methods of analysis, modify existing methods, and/or discuss quantitative and analytical approaches to data. They may rely on "highly technical materials" (APA, 2010, p. 11) and appeal to more experienced researchers. Finally, case studies are reports that illustrate a problem, provide solutions to the problem, and highlight the need for additional research on the problem, clinical applications, or theory related to the problem (APA, 2010). Other types of articles published in scholarly journals may include book reviews, letters to the editor, brief reports, program analyses, and monographs. These types of articles are usually refereed, or reviewed, by experts in the discipline of study. There is a plethora of these journals in criminal justice, but a few examples include *Youth and Society*, *Deviant Behavior*, *Criminal Justice and Behavior*, and *Criminology, Criminal Justice, Law & Society*.

It should also be noted that the term *journal* in the title of a publication does not necessarily indicate it is refereed (University of Washington–Tacoma, 2018). Nonrefereed or edited articles may appear in journals in print and online. Trade journals are usually considered nonrefereed or edited and are written by and for professionals in a particular field or industry. These types of journals are useful for content on current practices and programs in criminal justice and other professions (University of Washington–Tacoma, 2018). As stated previously, nonrefereed or edited journals use editors or editorial boards to review article submissions from authors. The editor or editorial board may or may not be familiar with the article's topic and typically review articles for grammar, relevance, timeliness, and style. If the article is seen as meeting the criteria, an editor can choose to publish the article in a nonrefereed journal. Although not the gold standard of publications, some articles found in edited journals are well written and contribute to the field or discipline in some meaningful way, such as those found in trade journals. However, students should not rely on these types of journals for solid, scientific content. A couple examples of edited journals include *Corrections Today* and the *FBI Law Enforcement Bulletin*.

Magazines

Magazines fall into the nonrefereed or edited category. Magazines are written for a general audience and do not necessarily follow academic style rules, such as APA formatting. Magazines may publish articles on many topics in one edition and may have paid advertising space for various products and services. Magazines are abridged, and the determination of what to publish is decided by an editor. Articles found in magazines are assumed to be factually correct but may contain errors and be written for universal appeal rather than truth. Examples of magazines include *Police Chief*, *U.S. News & World Report*, and *Newsweek*, among others.

Government Publications

Government publications tend to follow the style rules of the APA. Government publications typically are produced by the U.S. federal government or a foreign government. The Department of Justice publishes the majority of articles in the United States related to criminal justice, although some other departments within the federal government write articles or do studies in criminal justice too. Government publications are considered legitimate, academic (or scholarly) sources. They are reviewed by scholars in the field and undergo a rigorous editing process. Students can find government articles by searching federal government websites or using Google to search a broad topic. Google can limit the topic search to only governmental websites if *.gov* is added to the search bar. The Department of Homeland Security, Office of Juvenile Justice and Delinquency Prevention, Uniform Crime Reports, and National Institute of Justice Publications are a few federal departments that students can use to find articles related to criminal justice topics. Of course, there are many other federal departments and websites as well.

Books

Finally, books are often used as references in student research projects. Books are not refereed by experts in the field, though they may be reviewed by individuals with knowledge in the subject area. Typically, publishers, like Sage or McGraw-Hill, commission authors to write books and guarantee the authors lump sum payments or royalties from the sale

"WHAT I CALLED CREATIVE RECYCLING THE SCHOOL CALLED PLAGIARISM."

Source: Used with permission from T- (Theresa) McCracken

of the book. The authors may write the entire book, portions of a book, or only single chapters. Books can be used as legitimate references for research projects, but they are considered secondary sources, not primary. In most cases, students should seek primary or refereed journal articles to supplement their work and not rely solely on books.

In summary, APA formatting will likely be used in almost all publications discussed in this section. APA formatting can help students decide how much authority to afford to a particular publication. If the publication follows rigid APA style and the articles in the publication are found to be refereed, the student can rest assured that the information is well founded in scientific protocol. However, if the publication provides a mix of styles or little APA formatting, the student should likely question the contents of the work. Comprehending that APA formatting provides a way for authors to communicate ideas and research clearly to one another is significant in understanding a student's need to learn and use APA style rules. In addition to the communication goal, APA formatting plays a part in ethical and legal standards in publishing. In the next section of this chapter, ethical and legal standards are discussed in relation to APA formatting and publications.

APA Formatting and Ethical and Legal Standards

Following legal and ethical standards in writing is a requirement of scientific researchers. If a researcher fails to follow ethical guidelines set forth by the discipline, he or she may face scrutiny, the research may be disregarded, and the researcher's reputation may not recover, which would dampen future projects. Legally, a researcher is required to follow statutes governing research and, in the case of using human subjects, may have to get permission for the research from the federal office of Human Subjects Protections, the researcher's agency, or an educational institution's Institutional Review Board (IRB), which governs the legitimacy of research. Knowing and understanding these expectations is extremely important for the scholarly researcher and will be discussed in the following paragraphs.

Ethics

Merriam-Webster's Dictionary (2018) defines *ethics* as a set of moral principles. It is assumed that these moral principles guide an individual's behavior by helping them to determine right from wrong. Ethics are usually learned from the family, in school, in church, or in other social settings (Resnick, 2015). Groups can also have ethics or principles that guide their approach to moral issues or situations and provide a philosophy specifying how they will behave. This group philosophy is known as professional ethics when it governs behavior in a particular profession. Psychologists, doctors, police officers, and many other professions practice professional ethics. Scholarly researchers also use professional ethics founded in scientific protocol and recognized by the APA.

Just as ethics govern the behavior of professions and "establish the public's trust in the discipline" (Resnick, 2015, Para. 6), ethics in research accomplish five main goals: (1) Ethics promote knowledge, truth, and the avoidance of error; (2) ethics promote collaboration in research; (3) ethics hold researchers accountable for their work and to the public; (4) ethics build public support for the importance of research; and (5) ethics promote other social and moral causes such as human rights, legal compliance, and animal safety, to name a few (Resnick, 2015, Paras. 7–11). Thus, given the importance of ethics in research, it is expected that all researchers will be familiar with and adhere to the ethical standards identified within their discipline or profession and within the scientific protocol when conducting research. Typically, researchers can find these ethical expectations in their professional code of ethics and/or on government websites that provide research ethics. Box 6.3 shows the professional code of ethics for probation and pre-trial services officers stated on Federal Probation and Pre-Trial Officers Association website. The professional code of ethics for research is provided in Table 6.1 from the National Institute of Health.

Box 6.3

Federal Probation and Pre-Trial Officers Association Code of Ethics

AS A FEDERAL PROBATION/PRETRIAL SERVICES OFFICER,

I AM DEDICATED TO RENDERING PROFESSIONAL SERVICE to the Courts, the parole authorities and the community at large in effecting the social adjustment of the offender and assuring the compliance of defendants with their legal responsibilities.

I WILL CONDUCT MY PERSONAL LIFE WITH DECORUM, will neither accept nor grant favors in connection with my office, and will put loyalty to moral principles above personal consideration.

I WILL UPHOLD THE LAW WITH DIGNITY and with complete awareness of the prestige and stature of the judicial system of which I am a part. I will be ever cognizant of my responsibility to the community which I serve.

I WILL STRIVE TO BE OBJECTIVE IN THE PERFORMANCE OF MY DUTIES, respect the inalienable rights of all persons, appreciate the inherent worth of the individual, and inviolate those confidences which can be reposed in me.

I WILL COOPERATE WITH MY FELLOW WORKERS AND RELATED AGENCIES and will continually attempt to improve my professional standards through the seeking of knowledge and understanding.

I RECOGNIZE MY OFFICE AS A SYMBOL OF PUBLIC FAITH and I accept it as a public trust to be held as long as I am true to the ethics of the Federal Probation and Pretrial Services System. I will constantly strive to achieve these objectives and ideals, dedicating myself to my chosen profession.

Revised March 11, 1993

Source: Federal Probation and Pre-Trial Officers Association. (2018). Code of Ethics. Retrieved from www.fppoa.org/page/code-ethics.

Table 6.1 Shared Values in Scientific Research	
Honesty	convey information truthfully and honoring commitments
Accuracy	report findings precisely and take care to avoid errors
Efficiency	use resources wisely and avoid waste
Objectivity	let the facts speak for themselves and avoid improper bias

Source: Steneck, N. H. (2007). *ORI.* Washington, DC. U.S. Government Printing Office, p. 3.

Introduction to the Responsible Conduct of Research

Ethics in scientific protocol provides basic standards for all researchers to follow when conducting and presenting research. According to scientific protocol (Smith, 2003), when completing ethical research projects, researchers should do the following:

1. *Be truthful in discussing intellectual property.* Researchers should discuss who gets credit for the work, how authors' names will appear on projects, and what work will be done by each participant. Faculty, independent researchers, and students who share in the responsibility of contributing to the conceptualization of the project, development and completion of the project, and distribution of the research deserve authorship and acknowledgment. Researchers also need to fulfill the ethical obligation of correcting research errors and/or allowing others to duplicate the research using the same data.
2. *Understand roles.* It is important for researchers to realize they play multiple roles in relationships. For example, a teacher who uses students in experiments may unintentionally violate the student's right to say no to the project because students may feel pressured: If they don't participate, their grade may be affected. Research participation should be voluntary for subjects. So, researchers should not take advantage of their professional role in pursuing research or research participants and should realize that the multiple roles they play in relationships with others could create a harmful or unethical environment for research.
3. *Show respect for persons.* As mentioned above, participants in research projects should participate voluntarily and without fear of harm. Research participants should know and understand the risks and benefits of the research, the purpose of the research, the expectations on their time and involvement, their ability to withdraw or refuse to participate, how their information and contributions will be identified, analyzed, and dispersed, if incentives are available for their participation, and who to contact if they experience discomfort or have questions. Researchers

should get consent to participate in research in writing from subjects and should continually assess the research to ensure it is not harming participants beyond what was identified at the beginning of the project.

4. *Protect confidentiality and privacy.* Like doctors are required to secure medical records, researchers have an ethical responsibility to protect the responses and identity of those who participate in research projects. Researchers should discuss with participants how their identity will be protected and when or if their information will be shared in publications or presentations. Researchers should talk to subjects about the harms they may experience as a result of their participation and should strive to eliminate as many of those harms as possible by securing the identity of research subjects. If a subject's name or other identifying information cannot be anonymous, the researcher should design a system to secure data in locked cabinets or behind security passwords on electronic devices. These procedures should be shared with the subjects, and their consent to participate once knowing the risk should be secured prior to involvement in the research project.
5. *Use other ethical resources.* A researcher should know and understand state and federal laws with regard to research and using human subjects in research. Additionally, a researcher should get permission for the research from his or her IRB if one is available or through the federal Office of Human Subjects Protections.

In addition to the ethical guidelines above, the APA requires the open sharing of data among researchers. They suggest that researchers maintain their secured data for a minimum of 5 years. This allows other researchers to request permission to view or verify the data. It also allows for questions to be answered with respect to the accuracy of the data, analysis, and publication (APA, 2010). The APA provides further guidelines on publishing data, duplicating work in multiple journals or articles (this should be avoided) and publishing data piecemeal or parsing out data in various publications. Accordingly, the APA prohibits researchers from misrepresenting data from its original format and publishing the same data or idea in two separate sources. The association believes this gives "the erroneous impression that findings are more replicable than is the case or that particular conclusions are more strongly supported than is warranted by cumulative evidence" (APA, 2010, p. 13). Piecemeal publications, or unnecessarily splitting the findings across multiple articles, is also discouraged by the APA because it can "be misleading if multiple reports appear to represent independent instances of data collection or analyses" (p. 14) and the scientific literature, as a whole, could be distorted. Of course, there may be times that an author must limit the amount of findings presented in a single article because of journal constraints or because the research project is ongoing. In these instances, the researchers should acknowledge any previous work using the data or idea both in the article as well as in discussions with the journal or book editor. Not doing so could result in legal as well as ethical challenges for the authors. Both copyright laws and plagiarism, which will be discussed, apply in these cases.

Discussing ethical responsibilities and understanding the potential ethical violations that may occur in a project beforehand is good practice for researchers. Being familiar with federal mandates on research ethics, like those from the National Institutes of Health, manuals, like the APA Manual (2010), and documents like *The Belmont Report*, a 1979 report from the National Commission for the Protection of Human Subjects of Biomedical and Behavioral Research, that discussed ethical practices in using human subjects and is still the basis for ethical practices in research involving human subjects, are key in avoiding ethical violations and determining how best to handle those that may occur.

Notice that being truthful is an essential element of research. For those researchers who choose not to follow ethical guidelines, legal issues may arise.

Legal Aspects

Writers must also be aware of legal issues that govern publications. Copyright and fair use laws, plagiarism, and protecting the health and welfare of research subjects are some of the legal concerns that researchers must consider when completing papers, presentations, research projects, and other works. As discussed in Chapter 2, copyright and fair use laws are federal laws governed by the U.S. Copyright Office and apply to original works. You will likely recall that these statutes do not apply to ideas, facts, systems, or methods of operation. One example of a common copyright error made by students is to copy and paste charts or graphs from outside sources into their work. This is inappropriate since the chart or graph is likely copyrighted. Using the original work or paraphrasing (i.e., summarizing in their own words) the original work without giving credit to the author is a potential violation of copyright laws and could possibly result in a lawsuit by the original author. If proper credit, such as citations and references, are provided acknowledging where the information came from, the student is typically on safe ground.

Fair use laws are part of the copyright law that allows nonprofit and educational institutions to reproduce original works, develop spin-offs of original works, and distribute copies of original works through sale or lease. Fair use laws also control public domain information. Public domain information includes material with expired, forfeited, or waived property rights, and where property rights do not apply, such as in government documents. Finding oneself in violation of any of the copyright laws or clauses could result in a number of legal penalties, to include fines ranging from $200 to $150,000 for each violation, an actual dollar amount for damages, having to pay attorney fees and court fees, jail, impounding of the illegal work, and injunctions (Purdue University, n.d.). Since student writers and researchers often do not have the resources to pay fines and court costs, providing credit when credit is due is the easiest way to avoid copyright infringements. Additionally, it is an ethical requirement. Aside from civil and criminal legal ramifications, it is considered plagiarism to not provide credit to original authors.

Plagiarism

Although there are no state or federal laws against plagiarism, there can be consequences for plagiarizing and, in extreme cases, civil liability may be one result. Plagiarism is using the words or ideas of another without affording proper credit to the original author. The APA Ethics Code Standard 8.11, forbids authors from claiming the words or ideas of another as their own (APA, 2010). Using only a few words, full sentences, or entire works in a paper or presentation without affording the original author the credit makes it appear that the writer created the work. This is an example of plagiarism. Self-plagiarism is also unethical and includes using previously published or submitted work as new scholarship. For example, a student who submits a paper in one class that was already submitted and graded in another class commits self-plagiarism. In yet another example, an author who submits a previously published article to a different journal has committed self-plagiarism. To avoid self-plagiarism "the core of the new document must constitute an original contribution to the knowledge, and only the amount of previously published material necessary to understand that contribution should be included [in the new work]" (APA, 2010, p. 16). Additionally, when using previously published or submitted work, the author's own words should be cited, and references should be made to the fact that the work was used previously. The writer should say things like "as I stated previously" or "as I published previously" to inform the readers that the material has been used before. The writer should also provide in-text citations that include his or her own name and the date the previous paper or article was published or submitted.

Committing plagiarism can result in hefty consequences. In 2003, a news reporter from the *New York Times*, Jayson Blair, was accused of plagiarizing 36 of the 73 articles he wrote for the newspaper. He copied words or stories from other news outlets, faked photos, committed self-plagiarism, and made up facts and quotes in many of the stories (CNN.com, 2003). As a result of his transgressions, he was fired from the newspaper and a very public investigation and article appeared in the paper describing what he had done. Blair has never worked in journalism again (CNN.com, 2003). Other cases of plagiarism have resulted in similar fates for journalists and book authors. One book author, Kaavya Viswanathan, was accused of plagiarizing portions of her book from other authors in the same genre and had a book deal worth more than half a million dollars revoked (Bailey, 2012). Viswanathan also changed careers as a result of the accusations. Students in college who commit plagiarism may also face severe penalties that include zero grades on papers or projects, referrals to academic dishonesty investigatory boards within the university, failing a class, and/or expulsion from the university, depending on the severity of the plagiarism. Box 6.4 presents Harvard University's student code of conduct with regard to plagiarism. Notice that the university refers to plagiarism as academic dishonesty and places the responsibility for upholding academic integrity upon the student. This is common practice for all writers, regardless of status (e.g., researchers, vfaculty, authors, students). It is the author, not the publisher, who is responsible for avoiding plagiarism.

Box 6.4

Tips to Avoid Plagiarism

Writers are required to differentiate their own words from those of others. They are required to format papers in such a way that a reader can identify a source used by the writer and to format information according to standard style rules. These style rules include APA, MLA, or *Chicago Manual of Style* guidelines.

It is considered plagiarism if a writer fails to acknowledge the work of another, claims—intentionally or unintentionally—the words or ideas of another, incorporates facts from another's work, or uses language written by another without providing the proper credit to the original author (Harvard Extension School, 2017–2018). Plagiarism in an academic environment can result in very serious consequences.

Harvard University places responsibility for avoiding and for identifying plagiarism on both faculty and students. Students are responsible for knowing and understanding the policies on academic integrity and for using sources in responsible ways. Harvard does not provide leniency for students who claim not to understand the rules and for those that "fail to uphold academic integrity" (Harvard Extension School, 2017–2018). Faculty are also responsible for paying close attention to work submitted by students and reporting violations of academic integrity and cheating to the dean of students.

Harvard, like many other schools, provides failing course grades for students who violate cheating and plagiarism policies. They may also suspend students for one academic year.

According to the Harvard Extension School (2017–2018), students can use the following tips to avoid plagiarism:

1. Cite all sources—this includes primary and secondary sources as well as online, open source, and instructor lectures.
2. Make sure to understand the assignment and its requirements—make sure the instructor wants outside sources to be included in the assignment and make sure to use the proper citation style
3. Do not procrastinate—waiting to the last minute to complete the assignment may allow for citation mistakes to occur. Work ahead and take the time necessary to avoid plagiarism.
4. Make sure to include all sources and be thorough—even when writing draft assignments, be sure to include all sources used to paraphrase, draw ideas, and quote. Put sources into the paper and the bibliography as it is written, not at the end.
5. Use your own words as much as possible—rather than rely on quotes and the words of others, students should "actively engage with the [intellectual] material" rather than stringing together long quotes from other scholars (Harvard Extension School, 2017–2018).

Source: Adapted from Harvard Extension School. (2017–2018). Tips to avoid plagiarism. Retrieved from https://www.extension.harvard.edu/resources-policies/resources/tips-avoid-plagiarism.

The Protection of Human Subjects

Finally, a legal issue confronting researchers is the protection of human subjects. The APA requires researchers to meet certain ethical requirements when using human subjects in research projects. These guidelines include the following:

1. Seeking university approval for the study
2. Getting informed consent from research subjects to participate in the study
3. Obtaining informed consent for recording voices or using images in the study
4. Taking steps to prevent individuals who withdraw or refuse to participate and protecting those that are clients, subordinates, and student participants
5. Only failing to use informed consent when certain factors are met (i.e., data collection is anonymous, where no harm or distress is involved for participants, and where no federal, legal, or institutional regulations exist)
6. Avoiding offering excessive inducements to coerce research participation
7. Avoiding deception in the research, especially if there is the potential for harm or distress for human subjects
8. Providing a debriefing for participants
9. Humanely providing, caring for, and disposing of any animals that participate in research studies (APA, 2018)

Exercise 6.1

You are a student in a criminal justice class. Your professor requires a survey study of 15 undergraduate students on drug use and abuse. Since human subjects will be involved in the study, what steps or procedures should you take to ensure the protection of their rights and welfare? What are your school's IRB requirements?

APA format suggests that authors include descriptions of how they accomplished these guidelines in any papers or presentations resulting from their studies. Additionally, the association suggests that protecting the confidentiality of research participants is the primary responsibility of the researcher. To protect confidentiality, the researcher should avoid "disclosing confidential, personally identifiable information concerning their patients, individual or organizational clients, students, research participants, or other recipients of their services" (APA, 2018). To protect confidentiality, a researcher can allow the participant to read and consent to the written material once the data have been analyzed and summarized and/or the researcher can disguise some aspect of the participant, such as changing their name, altering characteristics, limiting descriptions of characteristics, using composites, or adding extraneous information to the descriptions (APA, 2010, p. 17).

Additional methods of protecting human subjects are provided by educational institutions and government entities that play a part in research that uses human participants. These bodies mandate IRBs that provide for the ethical and regulatory oversight of research projects. IRBs have the ability to approve, make modifications to, and reject research proposals that involve human subject participation. Fundamental in their role is to ensure that human subjects are humanely treated and that their rights and welfare are protected during the study's duration. The IRB reviews research protocol and other materials prior to the beginning of the study and before any humans participate to make their determinations regarding appropriateness. Legal mandates, like those published in the *Federal Register* (2018), require IRB reviews for studies funded by federal agencies. Universities, although not federally mandated to have IRBs unless they participate in federally funded research, usually require students and faculty to seek IRB approval before participating in projects involving human subjects. Not doing so can result in sanctions for the student and/or faculty member and, in the case of funded research, revocation of the funding and termination of the research project. Thus, researchers planning a study using human participants should become familiar with their institution's IRB standards and review procedures.

Exercise 6.2

What would you do if you knew a student in your class was selling papers to other students to submit for grades in a course. Is this an ethical or legal violation? Why or why not? Since you know of the infraction, can you be held accountable if you choose not to do anything?

Typically, the review process is similar across all institutions and includes an application, a review, and a decision. The application asks researchers to identify the research project, hypothesis, methods, and methodology, as well as specific characteristics about the human subjects to be recruited, their participation expectations, harms, duress, rewards, and debriefing procedures. Other questions and documents, like the informed consent forms, may be required with the application and used to determine if the rights and welfare of the subjects are protected (*Federal Register*, 2018). If the researcher is not using protected groups, such as prisoners, pregnant women, children, in vitro fertilization, or mentally incompetent persons, the IRB may choose to use an expedited review process where only one or two members of the board review the application and make a decision. If, however, protected groups are being recruited for the study, a full board review will be required before a decision can be made to approve, modify, or disapprove of the research application (*Federal Register*, 2018). The review process can take several months, so researchers should consider this when preparing to complete a research study.

In summary, research is guided not only by the ethical standards developed by the APA, but also by legal and ethical expectations set by the federal government and educational institutions. Students in criminal justice are expected to know and understand the importance of using a uniform style of writing to present research and to follow the "sound and rigorous standards of scientific communication" (APA, 2010, p. xiii). The APA sets this style and provides a format, or simple set of rules (e.g., style rules), to facilitate reading comprehension in the social and behavioral sciences. Found in the *APA Publication Manual*, the style rules provide a model of writing across many social science disciplines and bring together the diverse approaches and scholarship for the benefit of readers and scientific literature, in general.

Modern Language Association and the *Chicago Manual of Style*

This chapter would be remiss if two additional styles of writing were not mentioned, albeit briefly. As discussed in detail earlier, the APA format is the most widely accepted style in social and behavioral science writing; however, two other styles of writing are sometimes used in journals, magazines, and at educational institutions. These styles are the MLA and the *CMOS*.

Modern Language Association (MLA)

The MLA was founded in 1883 and is the most frequently used formatting style in the humanities and liberal arts (MLA, 2018). The MLA hosts national conferences and an informative website for style rules and formatting. With more than 25,000 members, the MLA has worked to "strengthen the study and teaching of language and literature" (MLA, 2018, no page). Like APA format, the MLA has established writing guidelines for formatting, page layout, abbreviations, footnotes, quotations, citations, and preparing manuscripts for publication. It also includes guidelines for plagiarism. Unlike APA format, which provides very specific style rules for almost every type of source in a lengthy manual, the MLA uses a core elements approach to citing sources. In this approach, writers only need to identify nine elements in each source:

1. Author
2. Title of source
3. Title of container
4. Other contributors
5. Version
6. Number
7. Publisher

8. Publication date
9. Location (MLA, 2018)

Once the writer has identified these core elements, he or she can use this format for basically any type of resource. If the source is a smaller work inside of a larger work (i.e., a poem in a book of poetry), the writer should consider the smaller work (poem) the source, while the larger work (book of poetry) is the container. The container is identified in the core elements as is the smaller work. Those interested in MLA style format can visit the MLA website at www.mla.org for more information.

Chicago Manual of Style (CMOS)

Last, but certainly not least, is *CMOS*. This style of writing is normally used in history and a few social sciences. This style uses two formats when citing resources. The first is the notes and bibliography system, which relies on footnotes and endnotes to create references to sources used in papers. In this system, the quote or paraphrase is numbered, and the corresponding number is placed at the end of the page or within a list of references with the full information needed to locate the source. The second system is an author–date system, where the author's name is found first in a reference and the date is placed last in the reference. More information on the systems used by *CMOS* can be found in the manual or online at www.chicagomanualofstyle.org/home.html.

The main differences in the three styles of writing—APA, MLA, and the *CMOS*—is where the emphasis is placed on citing sources and references and which disciplines use the style. APA format is most commonly used in the social sciences and places emphasis on the date the work was created. The date of publication is placed in in-text citations immediately following the quote or paraphrase and immediately after the author's name in the references. The most recent style rules for APA format can be found in the newest edition of the *APA Publication Manual* on the APA website at www.apastyle.org and on the Purdue OWL: APA Formatting and Style Guide at https://owl.purdue.edu/owl/research_and_citation/apa_style/apa_formatting_and_style_guide/general_format.html. MLA is primarily used in the humanities and liberal arts and emphasizes the authorship of the work. The author's name is placed in in-text citations in the body of the paper, and the author's name is found first in the references section of the paper. MLA uses core elements to format citations that apply to almost any type of source. The formatting can be found in the newest edition of the MLA manual. Last, *CMOS* is used by some social sciences, but mostly in history. The *CMOS* uses two types of citation and reference styles: a notes and bibliography system and an author–date system. The notes style is generally used by history and relies on footnotes and endnotes when citing sources. The *CMOS* latest guidelines can be found in the manual. Even though there are multiple formats of writing, students in criminal justice use APA formatting and follow the ethical and legal standards put forth by the APA *Publication Manual*, universities, and federal mandates.

CHAPTER SUMMARY

Regardless of the writing system used, formatting and writing style are important to simplify the writing process for the author and to make things easier for the reader. By following standard guidelines in writing, authors within disciplines can more easily create and publish works for general consumption and for use in academic scholarship. The rules in which they design their research are agreed upon by all within the discipline so researchers can focus on the essence of the research. Thanks to style rules, readers can effortlessly identify sources within written documents and can read for understanding rather than worrying about the style rules of grammar, citation, referencing, graphing, etc. In the social sciences, particularly, criminal justice, the APA sets the style rules followed by researchers, writers, and publishers.

In addition to general style rules, the APA provides guiding principles in research and writing ethics. Federal government offices provide legal mandates on research, and universities comply with both the ethical and legal standards by reviewing and ensuring that students and faculty are following the laws, protecting human subjects, and providing credit for works used in their investigations. Individuals found to violate the ethical or legal directives may find that they experience civil or criminal penalties and/or are ruined as writers, authors, or researchers.

QUESTIONS FOR CONSIDERATION

1. Why is it important to protect human subjects involved in academic research?
2. Identify the most pressing ethical issue in social science research, in your opinion.
3. What is the definition of plagiarism? What is the difference between plagiarism and self-plagiarism?

CHAPTER 7

The Academic Research Paper

Many students cringe at the very thought of writing a research paper. It is often viewed both by strong writers and those who lack confidence in their writing skills as a tedious, boring assignment that requires a great deal of time to complete. This chapter will introduce students to conducting research, locating and evaluating sources, reading scholarly journal articles, and writing a research paper using credible sources. The chapter includes sample student essays. With the guidance contained in this chapter, students should no longer dread a research paper assignment.

The Research Writing Process

The research paper is similar to other kinds of essays, "the difference being the use of documented source material to support, illustrate, or explain" the writer's ideas (Wyrick, 2013, p. 371). It is "a documented essay containing citations to the source you have consulted (that) combines your own ideas, experiences, and attitudes with supporting information provided by other sources" (Schiffhorst and Schell, 1991, 325). Readers may also find your resources useful to their research of similar topics.

Create a Realistic Schedule

Writing well takes time, so plan your time well. Always begin by setting a realistic schedule for completing the essay, taking account for the responsibilities and activities in your life, such as other classes and assignments, home life, work, and social time. Consult the course syllabus and review the course policies for submitting assignments. Many professors will not accept late submissions or significantly lower the grade for late work. It is always safest to treat the assignment due date as an absolute deadline with no option for submitting the paper late.

Students will usually have several weeks to complete an essay assignment, but do not fall into the procrastination trap by putting things off that are not immediately due. Start planning and brainstorming topic ideas as soon as the assignment is received. Allow time for brainstorming, researching, drafting, and revising, revising, revising, and pay close attention to drafts or other assignments due before the research essay's final due date.

Finally, print or create a paper copy of the schedule and post it in a conspicuous place to serve as a constant reminder. A sample schedule based on a five-page research essay is shown on the next page.

Table 7.1 Sample Paper-Planning Schedule

Task	Required Time	Due Date
Research essay assignment received from professor on		Assigned on Aug. 20
Brainstorm topic ideas	1 hour	
Quick Internet search to ensure source material is readily available	1 hour	
Research	3 hours (minimum—more for longer assignments)	
Writing, Rough Draft 1	5 hours	
Submit Draft 1		**Due Sept. 3**
Writing, Rough Draft 2	3 hours	
Submit Draft 2		**Due Sept. 10**
Research	2 hours	
Writing, Create References page	1 hour	
Writing, Final Draft and editing	3 hours	
Submit Final Research Essay		**Sept. 16**
Total time based on a five-page essay	19 hours	

Select a Topic

A professor may assign the research essay topic, or a student may be free to select a topic. One way to make the research essay assignment more satisfying for the writer and interesting for the reader is to write about a familiar topic. "The best way to avoid . . . needless drudgery is to choose a subject you already know something about and want to learn more about" (Schiffhorst and Schell, 1991, p. 327). Consider choosing "something that interests you. You'll be spending a lot of time on this assignment, and you'll be happier writing about a topic that engages you" (Brown, 2014, p. 244). Take the time to fully explore the choices, making certain the topic satisfies the requirements of the assignment. It is always best to check with the professor for additional insight and final approval.

Focus the Topic

Inexperienced writers often choose an essay topic that lacks focus. If a student were to research police body cameras, for example, it would be impossible to read and evaluate the information contained in the thousands of web sites, journal articles, and databases that would be discovered.

Before beginning the research, develop some specific ideas on what the audience should know about the topic. An essay on police body cameras might focus on one of the following more narrow concepts:

1. Do police body cameras reduce use of excessive force incidents?
2. What is the effect of body cameras on community relations?
3. Can the use of body cameras reduce the number of misconduct complaints?
4. Is a citizen's right to privacy violated by the use of body cameras?
5. Can the use of body cameras increase the safety of officers and the public?

When considering a topic, make certain a sufficient body of literature exists to support your thesis. While an abundance of information about police body cameras can be easily located, little has been written about police accreditation. Despite its interest to the writer, choosing a topic without easily available and adequate resources will make researching and writing the research paper especially difficult.

Exercise 7.1

Each of the topic questions listed below are too broad for a research essay assignment. For each, list two or three ideas on how these topics could be focused into a more appropriate essay topic.

1. Do police officers use too much force?
2. Does segregation really protect inmates from violence?
3. Should all juveniles who commit a felony be charged as an adult?
4. What challenges does a felon face when seeking employment?

Conducting Research

Primary and Secondary Sources

Primary sources include research, publications, reports, interviews, and other original material (Schiffhorst and Schell, 1991). Secondary sources are created with the support of primary sources. Primary sources give a truer sense of the topic than any secondary source could provide (Bombaro, 2012). Collecting data for a primary source, though, can be challenging. Obtaining primary source data requires conducting individual or focus group interviews, completing survey research, or observing participant behavior, and the process can be both costly and time-consuming. Some primary source data collected by researchers is available on criminal justice databases. For example, a student researching family violence might consult a Bureau of Justice Statistics (BJS) report. The report is a primary source since it is based on crime statistics collected and analyzed by the BJS, and this information is essential to understanding the issue. Students should "locate and use as many primary sources as possible" (Schiffhorst and Schell, 1991, p. 336).

Secondary sources rely on interpreting primary or other secondary sources to support or counter the author's thesis. These include books, scholarly articles, and other documents authored by someone who did not conduct original research or experience the event firsthand (Brown, 2014). Students should evaluate secondary sources carefully for credibility. Companies and organizations often fund research with the intent of a pre-determined outcome. Information about evaluating sources is included later in this chapter.

Locating Sources

General Search Engines

The Internet is an important resource and should be a part of your research plan. With just a few keystrokes, a seemingly endless collection of information can be located. Google, Bing, and Ask are the most popular general search engines, but students should always be cautious of Internet information since anyone can post information to the Web (Ratcliff, 2018).

Search engines seek matches to search terms by scanning millions of Web pages (Hacker, 2006). General search engines can be a good starting point for research, and even Wikipedia can identify valuable source information. But general search engines should not be used as a primary source for information. Later in this chapter, we discuss evaluating the credibility of sources.

Use Search Parameters

Use search parameters to refine and focus a search:

1. Use quotation marks around words to search for and exact phrase: "police use of force."
2. Put - in front of words that should not appear in the results: police - Sheriff.**

3. Use OR if either of two terms should appear in the results: police or sheriff.
4. Insert "site:" in front of a word to search for websites or domains: Site: corrections.

Many search engines have an Advanced Search page for other search options. Google, for example, includes the following page to help focus a search:

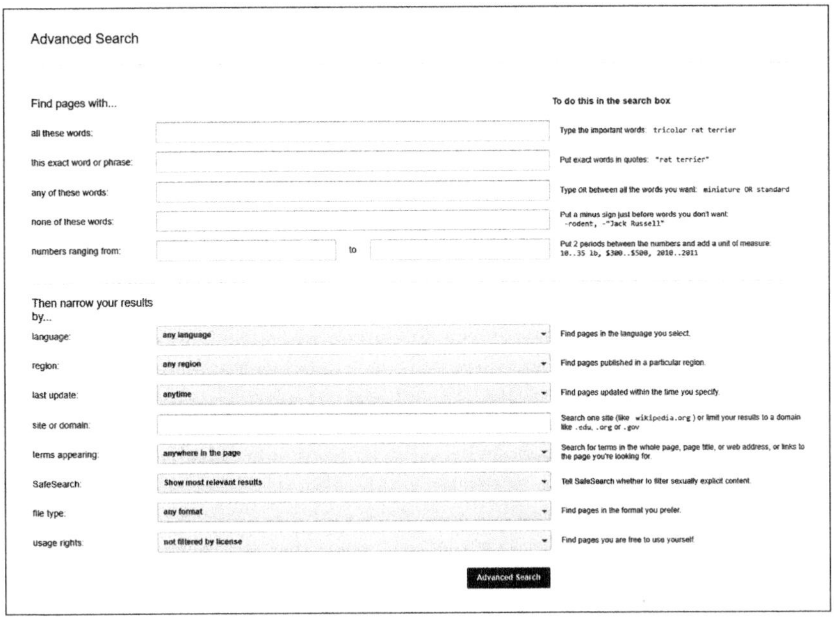

Note: Google and the Google logo are registered trademarks of Google LLC. Used with permission.

Google Scholar

Google Scholar (GS) can help focus a search since it omits general readership returns. Google describes the site as "a simple way to broadly search for scholarly literature . . . (such as) articles, theses, books, abstracts and court opinions, from academic publishers, professional societies, online repositories, universities and other web sites" (Google Scholar, n.d.). Anyone who knows how to use Google can effectively use GS to quickly access research articles completed by scholarly authors. Like any product, though, GS is not without criticism. Shultz (2007) suggests the advanced search function can be unreliable and that some returns may not be scholarly. Like any source, GS should be used cautiously by the researcher, and materials should be evaluated critically. Google Scholar should never be the sole source of identifying research materials, and it should never replace library databases. Nevertheless, GS can be an effective starting point for students to identify scholarly materials and authors. Cathcart and Roberts (2006) suggest GS is but one database and is best used "as a bridge to the more reliable, comprehensive resources offered by the libraries" (14).

Exercise 7.2

1. What name do the British use for the American Revolutionary War?

   Search: site: uk American Revolutionary War

2. What was the Russian name for the war on the eastern front in World War II?

   Search: site: ru wwII eastern front

3. How is gun ownership reported by United Kingdom and American news outlets?

   Search: site: uk US gun ownership, site: us gun ownership

See answers on p. 135.

Use Country Codes

According to Alan November (2016), the challenge of Internet research is in "learning how to access and synthesize massive amounts of information from all over the world. To manage overwhelming amounts of information, it is critical to learn how to design searches that take you past the first page of results" (para. 8).

Google's default setting is to search web sites in the region where the search originates. Whenever a student researches a problem that involves another country, they should use a country code to generate sources from that country (November, 2016). For example, perhaps a student wants to research differences in police use of force between the United States and the United Kingdom. Using the search terms "use of force" and "differences in US and UK policy" returns few results. But adding the search term "site:" and the country code UK (site: uk) focuses the search to UK sources and provides insightful information that might not otherwise be found. Adding "ac" to the search term, such as site: ac.uk, limits results to UK academic institutions. A list of country codes can be found at http://www.web-l.com/country-codes/.

Use Databases

Utilizing Databases

Criminal Justice Databases

Criminal Justice databases focus on issues related to crime, prisons and jails, probation and parole, juvenile justice, and the courts. The information located in these databases comes from journals, books, and government reports. Use these and other related databases when researching a criminal justice topic:

1. National Criminal Justice Reference Service (NCJRS): https://www.ncjrs.gov/index.html
2. National Archive of Criminal Justice Data: https://www.icpsr.umich.edu/icpsrweb/content/NACJD/index.html
3. Bureau of Justice Statistics: https://www.bjs.gov/

4. Federal Bureau of Investigations (FBI) Publications: https://ucr.fbi.gov/ucr-publications.
5. Criminal Justice Abstracts (Access through an institution or local library. See Library Databases).
6. JSTOR https://www.jstor.org/.

Students can find an extensive listing of criminal justice databases compiled by the University of Michigan at http://libguides.umflint.edu/c.php?g=428962&p=3263967.

Library Databases

Some databases charge a subscription fee and are not as straightforward to access as general search engines. Most college libraries and some public libraries subscribe to databases that provide unlimited access to scholarly resources not available on the Internet (Hacker, 2006). Databases like ProQuest, EBSCO*host,* and LexisNexis fall into this category. Check the library web site or ask a librarian about how to access these sites.

LexisNexis Academic

The LexisNexis database contains information collected from thousands of legal and news sources. Full-text publications are available from newspapers, legal news, magazines, medical journals, trade publications, transcripts, wire service reports, government publications, law reviews, and reference works (LexisNexis Academic, n.d.). LexisNexis Academic is available only by subscription.

Source: Abraham Baldwin Agricultural College Libraries. http://www.abac.edu/academics/baldwin-library.

Procon.org

ProCon.org describes itself as a "nonprofit, nonpartisan public charity (that) provides professionally researched pro, con, and related information on more than 50 controversial issues . . . by presenting controversial issues in a straightforward, nonpartisan, and primarily pro-con format" (About Us, n.d.). Students who struggle with selecting a topic will find the site's broad selection of timely and relevant issues to be an excellent starting point for the research paper.

Topics are introduced with a thorough summary followed by an easy-to-read, side-by-side debate of both sides of the issue. The site notes, for example, that police body cameras may improve officer accountability, while acknowledging the cameras may invade the privacy of citizens (Police Body Cameras, n.d.). Source information is well documented, and facts can be evaluated for accuracy.

Traditional News Sources

Although print and traditional TV news outlets have faded in popularity, newspapers and network news sources remain valuable sources of information for researchers. EBSCO (2018), a leading provider of databases and information sources to libraries, provides access to full-text newspapers covering national and international events. Transcripts from television and radio newscasts are also available. Many college and university libraries subscribe to EBSCO*host*, where students can access "nearly 60 full-text national and international newspapers and more than 320 full-text regional newspapers" (EBSCO, 2018, para. 3).

Benefit From Previous Research in the Topic Area

Students can benefit from the work of authors who have studied and published research similar to their topic. When a source is located, students should carefully read the Reference page paying particular attention to titles that appear to be closely related to their topic. The bibliographic information should be added to the Working Bibliography. Using the author's name and title of the work, search one of the earlier described databases until the source is located. It is always best to locate a full-text copy of the source. Students can read the full details of the work and evaluate its usefulness to their research essay.

Evaluating Sources

All source material should be evaluated thoroughly since anyone can post information to the Web. Using a plausible source can discredit an essay and the writer. According to Kirszner and Mandell (2014), students should ask four questions when evaluating sources:

1. Is the source *respected*? Peer-reviewed scholarly articles are valued much more than general readership articles. Likewise, a major news publication, like the *Wall Street Journal* or the *New York Times*,

is considered a more dependable source than an independent newspaper.

2. Is the source *reliable*? Reliable sources depend on factual, documented information that supports the thesis. In a reliable source, the author will include source citations that can be checked for accuracy.

3. Is the source *current*? Current sources provide information relevant to the topic. There is no standard for how old a publication might be yet still remain current. A technology article could be outdated in a year or less, while information on Community Policing from the 1980's might be current.

4. Is the author of the source *credible*? What other publications has the author written, and have they been cited by other researchers? Is the author employed by a company or foundation that suggests a particular bias? (pp. 760–761)

The use of credible sources is a sign of a well-written essay.

How to Read a Scholarly Article

Critically reading a scholarly article can be challenging for students. Even for students who are strong readers, the scholarly article is unique from other writing genres. The format, language, and data tables make it an "active, complex process of making meaning in which a reader draws information from several sources and concurrently constructs a representation of a text's message" (McLoughlin, 1995, p. 29).

Scholarly articles follow a specific format that includes an Abstract, Introduction, Literature Review, Research Methods, Analysis, Findings or Results, Discussion, and References. The Abstract appears at the beginning of the article and is usually limited to about 250 words. It is a summary of the problem examined by the author, an overview of the study, and the author's findings. The Introduction identifies the need for research in the topic area, identifies the focus of the study, and its relevance to the field, such as Criminology. In order to fully understand the issue, a Literature Review is included, which is the author's research in the topic area. The Literature Review is described in more detail later in this chapter. The Research Methods section includes information about critical aspects of the study: the data, the research sample, and a description of the statistical or other methods used to analyze the data. First, it is important to understand the source of the type of data to be analyzed. Is the data qualitative or quantitative? Qualitative data is numbers while quantitative data is text, such as subject interviews and observations of study subjects. Is the author using primary or secondary data, and how was the data collected? Next, it is critical to understand the unit of analysis. In other words, what exactly is the researcher analyzing: individual people, groups, criminal justice agencies or programs, or other outcome measures? Virtually anything can be analyzed. Finally, what methods did the author use in the analysis? The Analysis section is often the most difficult for students to comprehend. In this section, the researcher reports in detail the application of statistical methods or other means of data analysis and the outcomes of the data analysis. Charts, graphs, and other visual representation of the analysis are included in this section. In the Findings or Results section, the author interprets the results of the data analysis. In this section, the researcher applies the outcome of the analysis to the research questions and determines if the analysis supports or refutes those questions. Finally, the author summarizes the study in the Discussion section. Researchers often discuss the limitations of the study, if the findings add to the scientific literature in the field, and the need for future studies in similar areas not included in the study.

Successful students often employ a strategy when reading scholarly articles rather than using an approach similar to other reading assignments. If an English professor assigns Nathaniel Hawthorne's *The Scarlet Letter*, the most efficient approach to reading the text is to start at the beginning and continue straight through to the end. But this approach is often not the most effective way to the read a scholarly article. Students should first read the Title, Abstract, and Discussion. This will help the student determine the nature of the study, what the author intended to prove, and if the study was successful toward that end. Next, skim the Literature Review, Research Methods, and Analysis to understand how the study was conducted. Then reread the Results and Discussion sections closely. Then, students should scan the References section to identify other studies that may benefit their research. Lastly, students should make brief notes or annotations while reading the scholarly article with a particular focus on areas that might be useful to their research.

Writing a Literature Review

Scholarly articles and essays written for graduate-level criminal justice courses require the inclusion of a literature review. Professors who teach undergraduate courses may require a literature review as well. The literature review is a summary of what the literature says about a specific topic (Purdue OWL, 2018c). It is essential for a writer to understand the topic, theoretical perspectives, problems in researching the topic, and major controversies in the topic area of any research project (Adams, Raeside, and Khan, 2014). Reading as much of the available literature as possible is the only way to do this.

The abundance of literature in any topic area requires students to narrow the topic and focus the research questions so that identified literature in the topic area is itself as limited and focused as possible. That said, a search in most topic areas will return an abundance of potential sources. Reading source material will increase the student's knowledge in the topic area and lead to other potential source material. When reading, students should identify experts in the field and seek out their literature in the topic area. Reading will also reveal theoretical perspectives used to identify the type of data needed to answer the research questions (Adams, Raeside, &

Khan, 2014). Additionally, problems with researching the topic area may be identified when reading the literature. For example, Jacobs (1999) observed that no official data exist on criminal offenses committed by police officers. With this knowledge derived from the literature, scholars interested in researching this topic understand that locating data will be problematic to their study.

The literature review is a critical piece of a research project. Reading the available literature will improve the student's knowledge of the topic and may allow them to speak to topic experts. Perhaps most rewarding, though, is the feeling of inclusion derived from the connection between other scholars' work and your own. As noted by Adams, Raeside, and Khan (1999), writing the literature review introduces students to an academic community as someone "who can speak and write with confidence and authority on a specific research problem" (p. 39).

Writing the Essay

Presenting the information contained in a research essay in a clear and ordered fashion is essential to the essay's effectiveness. Students may find creating an outline of the essay's major points helpful in organizing the logical flow of ideas. Follow the outline, but do not be afraid to move information if it fits better elsewhere (Kirszner and Mandell, 2010). Every essay should be structured logically with a distinct Introduction, Body, and Conclusion.

The Introduction section is usually one paragraph in length, but it may be several paragraphs for longer assignments. The thesis statement is often the last sentence in this paragraph. It is a clearly written, single sentence intended to inform the reader of the writer's main idea.

Body paragraphs support the thesis statement. The writer's ideas are supported by paraphrases and quotations from sources and the writer's opinion (Kirszner and Mandell, (2010). Each paragraph should begin with a clear topic sentence using language identical or similar to the thesis statement and focus on a single idea. The last sentence of each Body paragraph should be a transition sentence. This sentence signals the reader that the topic is about to change.

Finally, the Conclusion paragraph summarizes the essay. It should include a sentence that restates the thesis statement as a reminder of the writer's main idea. The Conclusion should be at least one paragraph, but it may be longer if needed.

Working and Annotated Bibliographies

A working bibliography is a list of sources you consult (Hacker, 2006). The working bibliography is the beginnings of the References list that appears at the end of the research essay and can be reviewed to relocate source material during the writing process. Researchers often locate many more sources than they actually use, so not all sources identified in a working bibliography will appear on the References list (Hacker, 2006).

The Internet makes creating a working bibliography a relatively simple process. All that is necessary is to capture the author's name, the title of the source, and the URL or reference site where the source was originally located. For example, a student researching the effect of prison architecture on inmate behavior on Google Scholar might locate a journal article titled "Prison architecture and inmate misconduct: A multilevel assessment." This information can then be copied and pasted into a Working Bibliography Word document and saved for later reference.

Clicking the quotation mark at the bottom of the source opens a new window containing the complete source information formatted in several reference styles. The APA format for this article is displayed below:

> Morris, R. G., & Worrall, J. L. (2014). Prison architecture and inmate misconduct: A multilevel assessment. *Crime & Delinquency, 60*(7), 1083–1109.

The annotated bibliography includes more detail than the working bibliography. An annotated bibliography includes the bibliographic details as well as a brief summary of the source content (Wyrick, 2013). The annotated bibliography serves several important purposes. For the student writer, "it demonstrates that you've read your sources and understand them, and it serves as practice for 'real' research" (Brown, 2014, p. 240). For other researchers, an annotated bibliography is a valuable resource. If an annotated bibliography is available in the researcher's topic area, time and effort can be saved in locating source information.

Prison architecture and inmate misconduct: A multilevel assessment [PDF] researchgate.net

RG Morris, JL Worrall - Crime & Delinquency, 2014 - journals.sagepub.com

Researchers have not yet devoted sufficient attention to the effect of **prison architecture** on inmate misconduct. Using data from the population of male prisoners in Texas, the authors explored the association between two **prison** architectural design types (as determined by ...

☆ 99 Cited by 72 Related articles All 8 versions

Source: Google and the Google logo are registered trademarks of Google LLC. Used with permission.

Exercise 7.3

1. Enter this URL into a web browser to access an annotated bibliography on women offenders prepared by the National Institute of Corrections Information Center: http://static.nicic.gov.s3.amazonaws.com/Library/021385.pdf.

2. Refer to the search parameters mentioned earlier in this chapter. Use a search parameter to locate an annotated bibliography on teen dating violence.

Figure 7.1 Sample Student Essay

Domestic Violence in Police Families

Student Name
College/University Name

Introduction

The vast majority of police officers go about the business of their profession in a proficient and honorable manner. Each year, millions of people who have contact with the police overwhelmingly report that officers acted properly and were respectful (see the Bureau of Justice Statistics series "Contacts Between the Police and Public," 1999–2008). Every profession, however, has rogue actors.

Despite a vibrant body of literature exploring police misconduct, few studies of crimes committed by police officers exist. Most are limited by a dearth of data or focus upon the actions of officers within a single department. Jacobs (1999) lamented that despite significant resources invested in the police and measuring crime, no official data on criminal acts committed by officers exists, leaving scholars, policymakers, and the public data deprived. The lack of data leaves scholars struggling to understand police criminality (Chappell & Piquero, 2004; Dunn & Caceres, 2010; Eitle, D'Alessio, & Stolzenberg, 2014), but the media are at no loss for dramatic accounts of officer misconduct. A simple Google News search for "police officer arrested" returns over 700,000 news reports, which may lead readers to conclude that crime committed by officers is pervasive and erode the public trust. Sounding official, the CATO Institute maintains the National Police Misconduct Reporting Project (see http://www.policemisconduct.net/), but it, too, is based on local news reports. Absent credible data, even scholars have turned to the news in search of information on officers involved in criminal acts.

Domestic violence committed by police officers

Few studies of domestic crime committed by police officers exist, but those that do suggest the frequency of domestic violence is at least as high as or higher among police families than the general population (IACP, 2003; Truman & Morgan, 2014). One study claims that 40% of police families experience domestic violence (Neidig, Russell, & Seng, 1992, p. 30), a rate more than twice that experienced in the general population (Truman & Morgan, 2014, p. 1). Another study suggests that in departments serving populations of over 100,000, 55% of agencies had a policy directed at handling domestic violence calls involving police officers (as cited in Erwin, Gershon, Tiburzi, & Lin, 2005, p. 14), suggesting police administrators recognize a problem exists.

Explaining domestic violence in police families

Several studies attempt to identify officer-level attributes that may contribute to domestic violence. One study identified demographics for those officers involved in domestic violence cases in a large, urban department. The majority of officers were minority male patrol officers with a mean age of 34 years. These officers had worked in policing for about 8 years and were typically assigned to high-crime areas (Erwin, Gershon, Tiburzi, & Lin, 2005, p. 15). Additionally, the authors found that most complaints (48%) were filed against the officer by the officer's wife, followed by the officer's ex-wife or ex-girlfriend (27%) and their present girlfriend (22%). Most complaints alleged simple battery (77%), and a number of officers had a history of at least one previous complaint of domestic violence (23%) (Erwin, Gershon, Tiburzi, & Lin, 2005, p. 17). Of the study group members, most were either immediately suspended (64%)

(*Continued*)

Figure 7.1 (Continued)

or arrested (26%). Just 8% of these cases, though, resulted in any final formal action due to a lack of support from the victim (61%) or a lack of evidence (31%; Erwin, Gershon, Tiburzi, & Lin, 2005, p. 17).

The impact of officer malpractice

Several studies suggest the media play a role in shaping public opinion. The great bulk of police work is isolated from the public's view, and much of what the public knows about the police is derived from the media (Dowler, 2003, p. 112). Repeated exposure to numerous media accounts of misconduct may lead viewers to believe the behavior is rampant (Weitzer & Tuch, 2004, pp. 308–309) and is strongly correlated with citizen perception of police conduct (Weitzer & Tuch, 2004, p. 321). Chermak, McGarrell, and Gruenewald (2006) found the more a person read news accounts of officer misconduct, the more likely they felt the officer was guilty (p. 272).

Responses to domestic violence by police officers

Perhaps most instrumental in revealing the problem of domestic violence acts committed by police officers was the federal Omnibus Consolidated Appropriations Act of 1996, otherwise known as the Lautenberg Amendment. The Amendment altered the Gun Control Act of 1968, which was designed to prevent the use of guns in domestic violence situations (Halstead, 2001, p. 2). Its most significant effect on police officers is that it removed the "public service" exemption, which previously allowed local, state, and federal officers to continue to carry and use firearms for employment-related duties (Halstead, 2001, p. 2). This retroactive act, though, made it illegal for anyone convicted of a domestic violence crime involving physical violence or a firearm, including police officers, to own or use a firearm (Johnson, Todd, & Subramanian, 2005, p. 3). This legislation forced agencies that may have previously ignored or informally addressed domestic violence within their ranks to identify past offenders and review and update agency policies on handling cases when the suspect is an officer (Johnson, Todd, & Subramanian, 2005, p. 3).

Conclusion

The purpose of this paper was to survey the available literature in an effort to better understand what is known about domestic violence in police families, its predictors, and the criminal justice system response to events when they occur. While few studies exist that examine domestic violence that occurs in police families, a number of studies suggest the rate of domestic violence committed by police officers may be higher than that of the general population.

While no profession is without its rogue actors, officers who commit acts of domestic violence must be dealt with swiftly in order to protect victims and the public trust. Successful policing is based on a relationship of trust between the police and the community they serve, for "without trust between police and citizens, effective policing is impossible" (U.S. Department of Justice, 1994, p. vii).

References**

About Us. (2018). ProCon.org. Available at https://www.procon.org/about-us.php#overview.

Barnett, O. W., Miller-Perrin, C. L., & Perrin, R. D. (2011). *Family violence across the lifespan: An introduction*. Thousand Oaks, CA: Sage

Blackwell, B. S., & Vaughn, M. S. (2003). Police civil liability for inappropriate response to domestic assault victims. *Journal of Criminal Justice, 31*(2), 129–146.

Castle Rock v. Gonzales, 545 U.S. 04-278 (2005).

Çelik, A. (2013). An analysis of mandatory arrest policy on domestic violence. *International Journal of Human Sciences, 10*(1), 1503–1523.

Chappell, A. T., & Piquero, A. R. (2004). Applying social learning theory to police misconduct. *Deviant Behavior, 25*(2), 89–108.

Chermak, S., McGarrell, E., & Gruenewald, J. (2006). Media coverage of police misconduct and attitudes toward police. *Policing, 29*(2), 261–281.

Dowler, K. (2003). Media consumption and public attitudes toward crime and justice: The relationship between fear of crime, punitive attitudes, and perceived police effectiveness. *Journal of Criminal Justice and Popular Culture, 10*(2), 109–126.

Dunn, A., & Caceres, P. J. (2010). Constructing a better estimate of police misconduct. *Policy Matters Journal*, Spring, 10-16.

** Partial Reference list

(Author created)

CHAPTER SUMMARY

This chapter introduced students to writing an academic essay using credible sources. Writing a successful essay begins with understanding the assignment due dates, including those before the final essay is submitted. Creating a writing schedule can help students meet these deadlines. Students should select a topic and focus the research questions on a topic area in which a sufficient body of literature exists to support the thesis. Literature can be found using primary and secondary sources identified through the Internet, library resources, criminal justice databases, and news sources. Students must critically analyze these sources for their respect as a scholarly source, as well as their reliability, currency, and credibility. By following the guidance contained in this chapter, students should find writing an academic essay a rewarding and educational experience.

ADDITIONAL READING

"Writing a Research Paper." Available at https://owl.english.purdue.edu/owl/resource/658/01/.

"Writing a Research Paper." Available at https://writing.wisc.edu/Handbook/PlanResearchPaper.html.

QUESTIONS FOR CONSIDERATION

1. The research essay is similar to other types of essays. What is a major difference between the research essay and other essays?
2. List and describe the four questions a student should ask when evaluating sources.
3. Define primary source and secondary source. Include a discussion of the advantages and disadvantages of each.
4. Discuss the advantages of using country codes for a search.
5. Visit a criminal justice database. Describe the information that can be found on the site and discuss how this information can benefit your research.

EXERCISE ANSWERS

Exercise 7.1 Answers

1. The American War for Independence
2. The Great Patriotic War
3. First page results for UK sites focus on gun control, while U.S. results focus on gun ownership.

References

About Us (2018). ProCon.org. Available at https://www.procon.org/about-us.php#overview

Adams, A., Kahn, H., Raeside, R., & White, D. (2007). *Research methods for graduate students and social science students*. Thousand Oaks, CA: Sage.

Administrative Office of the U.S. Courts. (1984). *The presentence investigative report*. Retrieved from https://www.ncjrs.gov/pdffiles1/Digitization/101715NCJRS.pdf

Albitz, R. S. (2007). The what and who of information literacy and critical thinking in higher education. *portal: Libraries and the Academy, 7*(1), 97–109.

Alleyne, R. (2011, February 11). Welcome to the information age—174 newspapers a day. *The Telegraph*. Retrieved from http://www.telegraph.co.uk/news/science/science-news/8316534/Welcome-to-the-information-age-174- newspapers-a-day.html

American Correctional Association Public Policy. (2017). Public policy on use of force. Retrieved from http://www.aca.org/ACA_Prod_IMIS/docs/GovernmentAffairs/ACA_PUBLIC_CORRECTIONAL_POLICIES_BOOK.pdf?WebsiteKey=139f6b09-e150-4c56-9c66-284b92f21e51&=404%3bhttp%3a%2f%2fwww.aca.org%3a80%2fACA_Prod_IMIS%2fACA_Member%2fdocs%2fGovernmentAffairs%2fACA_PUBLIC_CORRECTIONAL_POLICIES_BOOK.pdf

American Library Association. (2018). Digital literacy definition. Retrieved from http://connect.ala.org/node/181197

American Psychological Association. (2010). *Publication manual of the American Psychological Association* (6th ed.). Washington, DC: Author.

American Psychological Association. (2018). Ethical principles of psychologists and code of conduct. American Psychological Association Ethics Office. Retrieved from http://www.apa.org/ethics/code/

Andrew, D. A., Bonta, J., & Wormith, J. S. (2006). The recent past and near future of risk and/or need assessment. *Crime & Delinquency, 52*(1), 7–27.

Angeli, E., Wagner, J., Lawrick, E., Moore, K., Anderson, M., Soderlund, L., & Brizee, A. (2010, May 5). General format. Retrieved from http://owl.english.purdue.edu/owl/resource/560/01/

Association of College and Research Libraries. (2000). Information literacy competency standards for higher education. Retrieved from http://www.ala.org/Template.cfm?Section=Home&template=/ContentManagement/ContentDisplay.cfm&ContentID=33553

Astolfi, C. (2016). Case dismissed, inmate released due to bad search warrant. *Sandusky Register*. Retrieved from http://www.sanduskyregister.com/story/201610140035

Bailey, J. (2012). 5 famous plagiarists: Where are they now? *Plagiarism Today*. Retrieved from https://www.plagiarismtoday.com/2012/08/21/5-famous-plagiarists-where-are-they-now/

Baldick, S. (1996). *Oxford dictionary of literary terms*. Oxford, UK: Oxford University Press.

Baxter, D. (2016). Thousands of fake ballot slips found marked for Hillary Clinton. Retrieved from https://yournewswire.com/thousands-ballot-slips-hillary-clinton/

Biber, D., & Gray, B. (2010). Challenging stereotypes about academic writing: Complexity, elaboration, explicitness. *Journal of English for Academic Purposes, 9*(1), 2–20.

Bombaro, C. (2012). *Finding history: Research methods and resources for students and scholars*. Lanham, MD: Scarecrow Press.

Breivik, P. (2005). 21st century learning and information literacy. *Change, 37*(2), 20–27.

Brewer, M., & American Library Association Office for Information Technology Policy. (2012). Digital copyright slider. Retrieved from http://librarycopyright.net/resources/digitalslider/index.html

Brown, L. (2014). *How to write anything: A complete guide*. New York, NY: W.W. Norton.

Brown, T. (n.d.). Functional standards development for automated case management systems for probation. American Probation and Parole Association. Bureau of Justice Statistics. Retrieved from https://it.ojp.gov/NISS/iepd/446

Business Communication. (2018). The importance of the business letter. Retrieved from https://thebusinesscommunication.com/importance-of-business-letter/

California Board of State and Community Corrections. (n.d.). Reporting and record keeping. Retrieved from http://www.bscc.ca.gov/downloads/Lesson_Plan_Sample_D-redacted.pdf

CareerBuilder.com. (2017). Number of employers using social media to screen candidates at all-time high, finds latest CareerBuilder study. Retrieved from https://www.prnewswire.com/news-releases/number-of-employers-using-social-media-to-screen-candidates-at-all-time-high-finds-latest-careerbuilder-study-300474228.html

Carole, M., & Richard, L. (1988). The effect of word processing on the quality of basic writers' revisions. *Research in the Teaching of English, 22*(4), 417.

Cathcart, R., & Roberts, A. (2006). Evaluating Google Scholar as a tool for information literacy. Retrieved from https://fau.digital.flvc.org/islandora/object/fau%3A7550/datastream/OBJ/view/Evaluating_Google_Scholar_as_a_tool_for_information_literacy.pdf

Centers for Disease Control and Prevention. (n.d.). DES research: Deciding whether a source is reliable. Retrieved from https://www.cdc.gov/des/consumers/research/understanding_deciding.html

CNN.com. (2003). *New York Times*: Reporter routinely faked articles. *CNN.com*. Retrieved from http://www.cnn.com/2003/US/Northeast/05/10/ny.times.reporter/

Crossick, G. (2016). Monographs and open access. *Insights, 29*(1), 14–19.

Davis, M. S. (1999). *Grantsmanship for criminal justice and criminology*. Thousand Oaks, CA: Sage.

Deschutes County Adult Jail. (2015). Use of force in a correctional setting. Retrieved from https://sheriff.deschutes.org/CD-8-11-Use-of-Force-in-a-Corrections-Setting.pdf

Dissell, R. (2010). Words used in sexual assault police reports can help or hurt cases. *Plain Dealer*. Retrieved from http://blog.cleveland.com/ metro/2010/07/words_used in sexual assault p.html

Doyle, A. (2018a). How to format a business letter. Retrieved from https://www.thebalancecareers.com/how-to-format-a-business-letter-2062540

Doyle, A. (2018b). Tips for formatting a cover letter for a resume. Retrieved from https://www.thebalancecareers.com/how-to-format-a-cover-letter-2060170

Eastern Illinois University. (2016). Scholarly monographs. Retrieved from https://booth.library.eiu.edu/subjectsPlus/subjects/guide.php?subject=monographs

EBSCO. (2018). Newspaper source. Retrieved from https://www.ebsco.com/products/research-databases/newspaper-source

Ellison, C. (2010) McGraw-Hill's Concise Guide to Writing Research Papers. Available at https://books.google.com/books?id=xvS7fIX2h6kC&printsec=frontcover&source=gbs_ge_summary_r&cad=0#v=onepage&q&f=false

Ennis, R. (2011). *The nature of critical thinking: An outline of critical thinking dispositions and abilities*. Retrieved from http://faculty.education.illinois.edu/rhennis/documents/TheNatureofCriticalThinking_51711_000.pdf

Federal Register. (2018). Federal policy for the protection of human subjects: Delay of the revisions to the federal policy for the protection of human subjects. Retrieved from https://www.federalregister.gov/documents/2018/01/22/2018-00997/federal-policy-for-the-protection-of-human-subjects-delay-of-the-revisions-to-the-federal-policy-for#_blank

Flaherty, M. P., & Harriston, K. A. (1994). Police credibility on trial in D.C. courts. *Washington Post*. Retrieved from http://www.washingtonpost.com/wp-srv/local/longterm/library/dc/dcpolice/94series/trainingday3.htm?noredirect=on

Gale, P. (2014). Effective business writing: Top principles and techniques. English Grammar. Retrieved from https://www.englishgrammar.org/effective-business-writing/

Gallo, A. (2014). How to write a cover letter. Retrieved from https://hbr.org/2014/02/how-to-write-a-cover-letter

Garcia, A., & Lear, J. (2016, November 2). 5 stunning fake news stories that reached millions. *CNN Money*. Retrieved from http://money.cnn.com/2016/11/02/media/fake-news-stories/index.html

Garner, B. A. (2013). *HBR guide to better business writing*. Boston, MA: Harvard Business Review Press.

Georgetown University Library. (2018). Evaluating Internet resources. Retrieved from https://www.library.georgetown.edu/tutorials/research-guides/evaluating-internet-content

Google Scholar. (n.d.). About Google Scholar. Retrieved from https://scholar.google.com/intl/en/scholar/about.html

Goring, D. C. (1984). Fourth Amendment—Prison cells: Is there a right to privacy. *Journal of Criminal Law & Criminology*, *75*, 609.

Hacker, D. (2006). *The Bedford handbook* (7th ed.). Boston, MA: Bedford/St. Martin's.

Hancock, D. R., & Algozzine, B. (2016). *Doing case study research: A practical guide for beginning researchers*. New York, NY: Teachers College Press.

Haner, J., Wilson, K., & O'Donnell, J. (2002). Cases crumble, killers go free. *Baltimore Sun*. Retrieved from http://www.baltimoresun.com/bal-te.murder29sep29-story.html

Harrison, J., Weisman, D., & Zornado, J. L. (2017). *Professional writing for the criminal justice system*. New York, NY: Springer

Harvard Extension School. (2017–2018). Tips to avoid plagiarism. Harvard University. Retrieved from https://www.extension.harvard.edu/resources-policies/resources/tips-avoid-plagiarism

Harvey, W. L. (2015). Leadership quotes and police truisms. Retrieved from https://www.officer.com/training-careers/article/12057342/leadership-quotes-and-police-truisms#platformComments

Heitin, L. (2016). What is digital literacy? *Education Week, 36*(12), 5–6.

Hilbert, M., & Lopez, P. (2011). The world's technological capacity to store, communicate, and compute information. *Science, 332*(6025), 60–65. Retrieved from http://science.sciencemag.org/content/332/6025/60

Hudson v. Palmer (1984). 468 U.S. 517.

Hunt, E. (2016, December 17). What is fake news? How to spot it and what you can do to stop it. *The Guardian.* Retrieved from https://www.theguardian.com/media/2016/dec/18/what-is-fake-news-pizzagate

Jacobs, J. B. (1999). Dilemmas of corruption control. In M. A. Kleiman, F. Earls, S. Bok, & J. B. Jacobs (Eds.), *Perspective on crime and justice: 1998–1999 lecture series* (pp. 73–93). Washington, DC: National Institute of Justice, U.S. Department of Justice.

Karsh, E., & Fox, A. S. (2014). *The only grant-writing book you'll ever need.* New York, NY: Basic Books.

Kellogg, R. T. (2008). Training writing skills: A cognitive developmental perspective. *Journal of Writing Research, 1*(1), 1–26.

Kirszner, L. G., & Mandell, S. R. (2011). *Patterns for college writing: A rhetorical reader and guide.* Boston, MA, Bedford/St. Martin's.

Kleckner, M. J., & Marshall, C. R. (2014). Critical communication skills: Developing course competencies to meet workforce needs. *Journal of Research in Business Education, 56*(2), 59.

Kong, S. C. (2014). Developing information literacy and critical thinking skills through domain knowledge learning in digital classrooms: An experience of practicing flipped classroom strategy. *Computers & Education, 78*, 160–173.

Lanza v. New York (1962). 370 U.S. 139.

Larson, A. (2016). What is Megan's law. Retrieved from https://www.expertlaw.com/library/criminal/megans_law.html

LexisNexis. (n.d.). LexisNexis academic. Retrieved from https://www.lexisnexis.com/en-us/products/lexisnexis-academic.page

McLoughlin, C. (1995).Tertiary literacy: A constructivist perspective. Open Letter. *Australian Journal for Adult Literacy, Research and Practice, 5*(2), 27–42.

Melé, D. (2009). *Business ethics in action: Seeking human excellence in organizations.* London, UK: Palgrave Macmillan.

Merriam-Webster's Dictionary. (2018). Ethics. Retrieved from https://www.merriam-webster.com/dictionary/ethic

Minnesota Department of Corrections. (2018). Use of force and restraints. Retrieved from http://www.doc.state.mn.us/DocPolicy2/html/DPW_Display_TOC.asp? Opt=301.081.htm

Modern Language Association. (2018). Works cited: A quick guide. MLA Style Center. Retrieved from https://style.mla.org/ works-cited-a-quick-guide/

National Forum on Information Literacy. (2018). National forum on information literacy 1999–2000 report. American Library Association. Retrieved from http://www.ala.org/aboutala/national-forum-information-literacy-1999%E2%80%932000-report

National Institute of Corrections. (2018). History. Retrieved from https://nicic.gov/history-of-nic

National Institutes of Health. (2017). Rigor and reproducibility. U.S. Department of Health and Human Services. National Institutes of Health. Retrieved from https://grants.nih.gov/reproducibility/index.htm

Nordquist, R. (2018). What is business writing? Definitions, tips, and examples. ThoughtCo. Retrieved from https://www.thoughtco.com/what-is-business-writing-1689188

November, A. (2016). The advanced Google searches every student should know. Retrieved form https://novemberlearning.com/educational-resources-for-educators/teaching-and-learning-articles/the-advanced-google-searches-every-student-should-know/

Ober, S. (1995). *Contemporary business communication.* Boston, MA: Houghton Mifflin.

Office of Justice Programs. (2018). Edward Byrne Memorial Justice Assistance Grant Program. Retrieved from https://www.bja.gov/Jag/index.html

Paul, R. (1995). *Critical thinking: How to prepare students for a rapidly changing world.* Rohnert Park, CA: Sonoma State University.

Paulas, R. (2016). On the front lines of computer literacy. *Pacific Standard.* Social Justice Foundation. Retrieved from https://psmag.com/education/this-part-is-called-a-url

Phillips Jr., W. E., & Burrell, D. N. (2009). Decision-making skills that encompass a critical thinking orientation for law enforcement professionals. *International Journal of Police Science & Management, 11*(2), 141–149.

Police Body Cameras (2018). ProCon.org. Available at https://www.procon.org/headline.php?headlineID=005399

ProCon.org. (2018). About us. Retrieved from https://www.procon.org/about-us.php#overview

Purdue OWL (2018). Types of APA Papers. Available at https://owl.purdue.edu/owl/research_and_citation/apa_style/apa_formatting_and_style_guide/types_of_apa_papers.html.

Purdue OWL. (2018a). Annotated bibliographies. Retrieved from https://owl.english.purdue.edu/owl/owlprint/590/

Purdue OWL. (2018b). Literature review. Retrieved from https://owl.purdue.edu/owl/research_and_citation/apa_style/apa_formatting_and_style_guide/types_of_apa_papers.html

Purdue OWL. (2018c). Parts of a memo. Retrieved from https://owl.purdue.edu/ owl/subject_specific_writing/professional_technical_ writing/memos/parts_of_a_memo.html

Purdue OWL. (2018d). Resume workshop. Retrieved from https://owl.english.purdue.edu/owl/resource/719/1/

Purdue OWL. (2018e). Writing a research paper. Retrieved from https://owl.purdue.edu/owl/general_writing/common_writing_assignments/research_papers/writing_a_ research_paper.html

Purdue University. (n.d.). Copyright infringement penalties. University Copyright Office. Retrieved from https://www.lib.purdue.edu/uco/ CopyrightBasics/penalties.html

Quible, Z. K., & Griffin, F. (2007). Are writing deficiencies creating a lost generation of business writers? *Journal of Education for Business*, 83(1), 32–36.

Ratcliff, C. (2018). What are the most popular search engines? Retrieved from https://searchenginewatch.com/2016/08/08/what-are-the-top-10-most-popular-search-engines/

Resnick, D. B. (2015). What is ethics in research and why is it important? National Institute of Environmental Health Sciences. Retrieved from https://www.niehs.nih.gov/research/resources/bioethics/whatis/index.cfm

Rowe, S. E. (2009). Legal research, legal writing, and legal analysis: Putting law school into practice. *Stetson Law Review, 29,* 1193.

Rugerrio, V. (2003). *Beyond feelings: A guide to critical thinking* (8th ed.). New York, NY: McGraw-Hill.

Santa Clara County Sheriff's Office. (2017). Use of Force. Retrieved from https://www.sccgov.org/sites/sheriff/jail-reforms/Documents/UOF%20POLICY%2008292017.pdf

Schiffhorst, G. J., & Schell, J. F. (1991). *The short handbook for writers*. New York, NY: McGraw-Hill.

Shama, J. (2017, May 6). Disciplinary reports remain high as Davison County Jail population rises. Retrieved from https://www.mitchellrepublic.com/news/4262326-disciplinary-reports-remain-high-davison-county-jail-population-rises

Shultz, M. (2007). Comparing test searches in PubMed and Google Scholar. *Journal of the Medical Library Association, 95*(4), 442.

Smith, D. (2003). Five principles for research ethics. *Monitor on Psychology, 34*(1), 56. Retrieved from http://www.apa.org/monitor/jan03/principles.aspx

Stanford's Key to Information Literacy. (2018). What is information literacy? Retrieved from http://skil.stanford.edu/intro/research.html

Technopedia.com. (2018). Computer literate. Retrieved from https://www.techopedia.com/definition/23303/computer-literate

University of Washington–Tacoma. (2018). Criminal justice: Source types: Peer-reviewed and scholarly and more. Retrieved from http://guides.lib.uw.edu/c.php?g=344206&p=2319662

U.S. Copyright Office. (n.d.). Copyright in general. Retrieved from https://www.copyright.gov/help/faq/faq-general.html#what

U.S. Courts. (n.d.). Probation and pretrial officers and officer assistants. Retrieved from http://www.uscourts.gov/services-forms/probation-and-pretrial-services/probation-and-pretrial-officers-and-officer

U.S. Department of Justice. (1978). Law Enforcement Education Program. Retrieved from https://www.ncjrs.gov/pdffiles1 /Digitization/49697NCJRS.pdf

U.S. Department of Justice. (2001). Pretrial services programs: Responsibilities and potential. National Institute of Justice, Issues and Practices. Retrieved from https://www.ncjrs.gov/pdffiles1/nij/181939.pdf

U.S. Department of Justice. (2014). Georgia police officials and former deputy indicted by federal grand jury on charges of excessive force and obstruction of justice. Retrieved from https://www.justice.gov/opa/pr/

georgia-police-officials-and-former-deputy-indicted-federal-grand-jury-charges-excessive

U.S. Department of Justice. (2018). Grants. Retrieved from https://www.justice.gov/grants

VandenBos, G. R. (2010). Foreword. In *Publication manual of the American Psychological Association* (6th ed.). Washington, DC: American Psychological Association.

Walters, W. H. (2007). Google Scholar coverage of a multidisciplinary field. *Information Processing & Management*, 43(4), 1121–1132.

Ward, D. (2006). Revisioning information literacy for lifelong meaning. *Journal of Academic Librarianship, 32*, 396–402.

Webb, H. (2011). *Managing the use of force incident: For criminal justice officers, supervisors, and administrators*. Springfield, IL: Charles C. Thomas.

Weiler, A. (2005). Information-seeking behavior in generation Y students: Motivation, critical thinking, and learning theory. *The Journal of Academic Librarianship, 31*, 46–53.

Wertz, R. E. H., Fosmire, M., Purzer, S. Saragih, A. I., Van Epps, A. S., Sapp Nelson, M. R., & Dillman, B. G. (2013). Work in progress: Critical thinking and information literacy: Assessing student performance. Unpublished manuscript presented at the 12th annual American Society for Engineering Education Conference, Atlanta, GA.

Wikipedia: About. (2018). *Wikipedia.org. Retrieved from* https://en.wikipedia.org/wiki/Wikipedia:About

Writing Center of Wisconsin-Madison. (2018). Writing cover letters. Retrieved from https://writing.wisc.edu/Handbook/CoverLetters.html

Wonacott, M. E. (2001). Technological literacy. ERIC Digest. Retrieved from https://www.ericdigests.org/2002-3/literacy.htm

Wyrick, J. (2013). *Steps to writing well with additional readings*. Boston, MA: Wadsworth.